Walking Out of Winter

One woman's journey of childlessness,
widowhood, healing and new love.

Rose Mitchell

To the Praise and Glory of God, who is Perfect Love and Author of our Restoration.

"For whatever things were written before were written for our learning, that through perseverance and through encouragement of the Scriptures we might have hope."

Romans 15:4

"Blessed be the God and Father of our Lord Jesus Christ, the Father of mercies and the God of all comfort, who comforts us in all our affliction, that we may be able to comfort those who are in any affliction, through the comfort with which we ourselves are comforted by God."

2 Corinthians 1:3-4

Contents

Page v - Foreword

Page 1 - Introduction

Page 3 - 1. Let Me Introduce You to My Friend

Page 9 - 2. Let the Journey Begin

Page 17 - 3. All is Not as it Seems

Page 30 - 4. Faith Being Tested

Page 40 - 5. When a Plan comes Together..

Page 47 - 6. ...And Then it Goes Pear-Shaped

Page 63 - 7. Farewell But Not Goodbye

Page 70 - 8. Questions and Answers

Page 83 - 9. The Man from the Train

Page 95 - 10. Transparency: the Chips are Down

Page 102 - 11. The Golden Thread

Page 111 - 12. A New Chapter Begins

Page 124 - 13. The Big Day Approaches

Page 131 - 14. The Honeymoon is Over

Page 141 - 15. Pastures New

Pae 148 - 16. Final Thoughts

Page 156 - Notes

Page 157 - Acknowledgments

Page 158 - About the Author

Page 159 - Helpful Organisations and Charities

Foreword

"See! The winter is past: the rains are over and gone. Flowers appear on the earth: the season of singing has come, the cooing of doves is heard in our land'. (Song of Songs 2:11-12. NIV)

These beautiful and hope-filled words, are both the inspiration for the title of this book, as well as a reflection of the very moving story Rose tells.

It is first of all a deeply personal account of the pain of unexpected bereavement. At times the book is refreshingly raw, as Rose describes the different ways the death of her first husband impacted her, and others close to them. But woven throughout the heartache and questions (from before and after the loss), is the motif of hope, and of a God who never abandoned her, even if at times it felt like it. Indeed, a God who often showed up and demonstrated his love, in surprising ways!

I hope you'll find, as I did, that through her honesty and vulnerability, Rose skilfully draws you in to what she writes, so that you can often imagine yourself present with her, whether in a moment of great pain, or unexpected joy. One of the book's other strengths is the way Rose describes how life has subsequently worked out for her (not least through her second marriage to John), which isn't how it will be for others. This is because we each have our own unique life-journey to navigate.

But in that journey, as Rose shows in a number of different ways, whatever our situation and circumstances, we can all discover a future and a hope, as we allow ourselves to be open to God's love, made known most clearly through the gift of his son Jesus Christ.

'Walking out of Winter' may, as Rose says, have been a long time in the gestation, but I think it's all the better for that!

Bishop Chris Edmondson.

Bradford. September 2023

Introduction

Although I am a Christian, I was a 'worst case scenario' type of person; I didn't expect good things to last because of my failure to maintain perfection. Happily married to my young husband for almost seven years, we were trying to start a desperately longed for family. Then, one day, the thing that I most dreaded actually happened and my world came crashing down.

This is my story of how God gently took me by the hand and walked me out of Winter, healed my broken heart and showed me that He had not abandoned me, and would never desert me; that life's challenges are not punishments.

The journey of grief and bereavement is a very personal one. I had my own beliefs about how I would cope with loss, but God's path for me was often radical and challenging, not for me only, but for others who knew me and my late husband, Martin. The beginning of my journey was bittersweet, but I am grateful, for it has brought me understanding of God's love and grace.

Having spoken of my healing experience with various people over the course of three decades, and being recently prompted by several dreams, I believe it's the right time to share on a wider platform.

I hope my story will help and encourage even more people who have faced the painful loss of a spouse or partner, or the crushing disappointment of childlessness, and bring hope that God is able to do the unexpected and wonderful. God gave me the opportunity and freedom to love again and helped me to reconcile my thoughts regarding other people's opinions about this through His Word, which has been an invaluable guide and source of comforting reassurance and instruction throughout and beyond. Thirty something years on, we are expecting our second grandchild.

As one chapter ends, a new one begins...

Chapter One

Let Me Introduce You To My Friend

My first encounter with Martin was at a full immersion baptismal service at a church in Southport, Merseyside. It was my first experience of such an event. I went along with some people from the Elim Pentecostal church which I had just started attending - quite a change from what I had been brought up with.

I had been going along to the local Methodist church with some fellow students from my college. It was full of lovely, hospitable people and was very much what I was used to. However I had recently been dumped by a boyfriend and was feeling very emotional and weepy. I considered that I would be very conspicuous if I'd started sobbing in the Methodist service, but less so at the more informal Elim church!

I managed to hold myself together all the way through the service, and was glad of the joyful, ebullient praise and worship, even though I wasn't feeling it myself. It was only when the Pastor's wife, a petite gentle Irish lady, spoke to me and took me to meet her husband that I 'let it all out' and sobbed all over his Sunday suit! I was invited for tea and, subsequently, a few weeks later, to the baptismal service in Southport.

I found the whole experience incredibly moving and exciting. I had only been used to seeing babies christened. The symbolism of being washed of your old life and coming up clean and new set my heart racing - this was something I wanted to do! I was too shy to do anything about it there and then; I couldn't respond to the invitation of the pastor to go forward and be baptised right at that very moment, but it was something I wanted to get more answers to. I'd always felt there must be more to the Christian life than just going to church.

Martin was one of the baptismal candidates. He was wearing a gleaming white shirt. To be honest, he didn't stand out to me during the service, but afterwards his parents (who attended an Anglican church) invited people back to their home for some refreshments.

That's where I really noticed him, lying on the orange fireside rug, with his thatch of blondish hair, rosy cheeks and disarming smile. He was 16 years old, I was almost 19; to contemplate anything more than friendship would be cradle snatching! But he was someone I wanted to get to know, because, even for his young years he seemed so at ease with the world and peaceful in his own skin. I was not like that at all. I was nervous and anxious about things going wrong, about my perceived ineptness. I wondered if it could ever happen; would we ever become friends?

Some exciting things began to happen in the town. A youth club started up in the community centre where the Elim church met. Young people from all the local churches began to meet there on Friday evenings. It became more than a place to meet and play games. Young people started to have a hunger to learn more about God. It was truly a special time and the Holy Spirit began to move gently and beautifully in the lives of many young people.

I started going along. It was refreshing to be with people who were not part of college life - living in halls of residence can get a bit claustrophobic (although I had some good friends in college). Martin went along too, and so we started to get to know each other, although we were just mates and enjoyed being daft together (he would make up silly songs about me). I began to take myself less seriously and have fun as well as learning about God's love and things of the Holy Spirit. I was baptised at Wigan Elim Pentecostal church during my second year at college.

As time went by, I realised that something deeper was happening with my feelings towards Martin. It was absurd! I was so much older than him! He was still only 17 - not even officially an adult (even though he could drive and was working). Besides, there was a string of younger girls he could take his pick from. However, one evening he called round to my lodgings, we had a conversation and from then on we were 'an item'. Joy and ecstasy!

We married three years later, after I'd got my teaching qualification. We lived in a tied cottage attached to a village church - the rent was verger's duties and digging graves (both were Martin's responsibility). The first grave he had to dig was for a former classmate who had been killed in a motor bike crash. That was a tough job!

We spent much time decorating that seriously dilapidated cottage. Before we were married, Martin had lived there and I lived at his parents' house in the "Granny annexe". We were only there six months because, unfortunately, one Summer morning, Martin had an unprovoked altercation with the vicar, receiving a swipe from his clenched fist! I think the poor man must have been suffering with his mental health. We tried to keep it low key, but our neighbours were journalists for local newspapers. It was too good a story for them to pass up, so, against our wishes, they published the story and it got into the national press. It looked as if we'd given interviews, but we certainly hadn't. The irony was, we had to phone the vicar to apologise for all the bad publicity that had been created.

So, we had to leave our beautiful first home. The leader of the parish council, (who had also experienced the vicar's wrath), found us a council flat, (which also needed redecorating!).It was a first floor flat on the edge of the same village, and had beautiful views over farmland. The downside was it had no immersion heater tank. Hot water came by lighting a fire in the kitchen grate which heated the water in a back boiler. Coming home on dark winter evenings, after an hour's bus ride and a full day teaching, that was hard work. Electricity was supplied via a coin slot meter. We got to know our neighbours, Peggy and Stan on the ground floor, well as I was often popping down to ask if they could change a banknote for coins for the meter.

After renting for a year, we finally moved into our lovely end-terrace cottage a few hundred metres from the church Martin's parents attended. Life was good, although it involved a bit more painting and wallpapering. This time it felt different!

Now that we were settled in our home, we began to think about starting a family. It turned out not to be as straightforward as we'd hoped…

Chapter Two

Let The Journey Begin

Now that we had moved to our new home my journey to work changed. I no longer needed to rely on lifts (something which caused me early morning anxiety), or wait for the bus, praying I hadn't missed it. I was now able to walk up the road to the train station and get the train into Liverpool, getting off at Walton Junction to catch a bus to my school. Mike, a friend from church, also caught the train from that station, so it was lovely to have some company and be able to chat. The next station after ours was Town Green, and amongst the people who boarded was a tall, smartly dressed man who Mike knew. Mike told me his name was John. We never actually sat with him or talked to him, but would politely nod to him and carry on our conversation. Often, by the time we got to this station the seats were already filled, and John would have to stand and hold onto the overhead hand rail as the train wobbled and weaved along its track. Sometimes, I would observe this smart man and wonder what his wife was like and if he had children. I hoped that he was happily settled with a lovely home and family. It was time for me to start my family with Martin in our pretty and cosy new home.

So my mind was now focussed on babies and I started daydreaming of cuddling my sweet, rosy-cheeked infant. I began collecting a few bits and pieces for the nursery, but didn't go too overboard; I didn't want to 'tempt fate' - there you can see the flaws in my thinking, that always there was the possibility that things could go wrong. There was always the whisper in my ear, the grey cloud lurking on the horizon, the 'What if this?', or 'What if that?'. Nevertheless, we started our journey to parenthood.

I first thought I might be pregnant in the Summer of 1985. We had met up with friends who were on honeymoon. I kept needing the toilet and had faint waves of nausea. I was trying to hide these, although Martin did comment on my constant trips to the 'Ladies'. Excitement was building in me; could I be incubating a very special secret? I couldn't wait to do a pregnancy test. I would do one at home first, because this was something that was private. I didn't want anyone knowing the outcome, one way or the other, not even the pharmacist!

Back in the day, home pregnancy testing kits involved a measure of setting up and procedure. The urine sample was collected in a test tube which had to be placed on a stand. The stand incorporated a mirror which reflected the base of the test tube. If, after thirty minutes, a brown ring appeared in the base, you could begin to celebrate a new life.

I read the instructions over and over. I set up the equipment and placed it carefully on the shelf in the bathroom. I read the instructions again and readjusted the equipment to make sure it was absolutely in the right position for optimum results. I performed the task of collecting the necessary sample, and with shaking hands and trepidation in my heart, I placed the test tube on its stand and started the countdown. Thirty minutes seems like an agonising eternity to await such life-changing news. Pacing the floor, wringing the hands, praying, checking the clock, sighing. Checking the test tube again..........

There was no brown ring, or was there? Maybe just a very faint one? Maybe not. Was I imagining it? Confusion and disappointment after the big build up. Deflated, I decided I would wait a bit longer and try again in a few days. These tests were not effective before the first six weeks. I still had the symptoms, I still felt nauseous. I would just have to wait and see.

I didn't need another test! A few days later I had confirmation that I wasn't pregnant. It was not just like the usual monthly event. It seemed much more significant than that, and I was very emotional. Martin told me to stay in bed and called the doctor for a home visit. The doctor duly arrived, but he seemed quite dismissive, saying not very encouraging things like: "These things happen", "You've probably lost it, (the baby)". I was advised to stay in bed a few days and rest, then try again in a couple of months. It was all so matter of fact to him. For me, it felt like a failure, I felt like a failure! And now it was out that we were trying for a family and it hadn't worked. Our privacy was invaded, because people ended up finding out why I was not at work, or church meetings, and it just added to the burden of grief and sadness.

As I sat in bed, feeling useless and bereft, I decided to reach for my Bible. Maybe I would find some words of comfort and encouragement, a balm for my soul. I turned to the book of Isaiah and began to read from chapter 54

"Sing, barren, you who didn't give birth! break out into singing, and cry aloud, you who didn't travail with child! For more are the children of the desolate than the children of the married wife," says the LORD." (Is. 54:1)

I carried on a little further down the page

"Don't be afraid, for you will not be ashamed. Don't be confounded, for you will not be disappointed. For you will forget the shame of your youth". (Is. 54:4)

And as I carried on reading I came to verse 13

"All your children will be taught by the LORD, and your children's peace will be great." (Is. 54:13).

I could feel my heart welling up with hope; tears flowed freely as I whispered a thank you to God for His kindness in leading me to read those verses. I hadn't come across them before, but they were spot on for my situation. I **was** feeling ashamed that I couldn't do what was supposed to be a natural thing; I was confused and disappointed at what had happened, but God was showing me He knew all about it and was bringing me comfort and hope. Verse 13 was particularly interesting. Was God actually giving me an assurance that I would have children? I decided to tentatively hide that little gem in my heart. I would hold on to that thought and pray that it was indeed a promise for me. I metaphorically released my little foetus into the arms of Jesus - trusting that I might see him (?) one day. I don't know the gender of that baby, but I named him Thomas just from a sense of intuition. Life carried on. Martin, in his sunny, 'all will work out for the best' mindset continued working hard to establish his building business and I continued with my teaching job. I was still travelling to work on the train, but trying to pass my driving test to give me a bit more flexibility with travel arrangements. My nervous disposition was great financial news for my instructor. I needed many lessons!

Just after Christmas we went on a Christian ski-ing holiday to The Black Forest region of Germany. It was a long coach trip and ferry crossing. Martin, of course, full of enthusiasm and zest for life went straight off to conquer the snowy slopes with a bunch of people he'd met. I was ok with that, I didn't want to cramp his style; I was in a beautiful place I never expected to visit. I stayed back at base and shuffled around with the local toddlers on the nursery slopes, breathing in the pure clean air and enjoying the powdery, white perfection glistening in the sunlight.

There was one day, however, when I decided to ' bite the bullet'. What was the point of being here and not engaging in the obvious exhilaration of ski-ing. I couldn't say I'd been ski-ing if I hadn't actually skied. So, I donned my skis, picked up my poles and marched towards the ski lifts. My heart was racing, there was so much that could go wrong; failure and fear of foolishness were staring me in the face, so I stared right back at them! God always sends kind people to help, and I managed to get myself in place at the top of a modest slope. The lessons I'd been taught by the ski instructor actually worked, and I gently descended the mountain with no mishaps. In this moment, I broke through a mental barrier. If I could do this, I could do anything, including passing my driving test. Yes, I would persevere and succeed. A line had been crossed!

On a clear, starry New Year's Eve, we joined our fellow skiers to see in the new year with Black Forest Gateau and glasses of warm, spicy gluhwein. It was magical to be in such a place surrounded by lovely people. The future lay before each one of us - I wondered what was in store for Martin and me? Would there be three in our family next year? I believed I'd had a promise from God, and I was hoping that the coming year would see its fulfilment.

Chapter Three

All Is Not As It Seems

Well, the room I'd earmarked for the nursery finally got an occupant, but not quite what was expected!

In the early hours of the morning, tucked up in bed and sleeping soundly, we were disturbed by an abrupt knocking at the front door. I leapt out of bed to see who it could be. There were two police officers, rubbing their hands, their breath misty in the chilly night air. I also noticed a sheepish looking figure crouched in the cab of Martin's pickup truck. We went downstairs to greet them.

"Excuse me Sir, are you the owner of this vehicle parked outside?", the officer enquired. We affirmed. Then he asked if we were acquainted with the gentleman they had discovered sleeping in the cab. I looked at Martin, waiting for his response:

"Oh yes, we know Mick. It's ok officers, he can stay with us, that's fine. Thanks.", and with that, they went on their way and Mick came in. He was very grateful, especially as Martin hardly knew him at all. He'd met him a couple of times labouring on building sites, but he wasn't about to turn him away. Mick ended up staying with us for several months until his circumstances improved. He was joined, for a short while, by another young man down on his luck. It certainly made life interesting! Such was Martin's heart for people, I just had to go along with it. His generosity of spirit was beginning to rub off on me. He had affirmed me, and I was proud of his kindness to others.

Mick was going through some difficult times, his marriage was on the rocks, he desperately missed his children, but at least now he had a temporary base, and sometimes Martin would have some work for him. I won't pretend it wasn't challenging. I told Martin that if our circumstances changed, we would need that spare room back. I was holding on to that promise.

On the days Mick wasn't working with Martin he would stay at home and try to make himself useful. One day I came home weary from work, noticing the washing was dancing in the breeze on the washing line. "How thoughtful, Mick's done the washing", I thought. As I continued focussing on the washing line, I realised all was not well. Everything was considerably smaller than it should have been. Mick had boil washed some of my favourite clothes, and now they would fit a small child. I could feel frustration simmering up inside of me! I took a few more steps up the path to the front door. By the grace of God I managed to rein in my fury and casually mention that it had been kind of him to do the washing. I went into the garden and pulled the pegs off the clothes. Tenderly caressing each garment, I silently grieved my loss; then with a deep sigh of resignation went in to start cooking the evening meal!

Somehow, we had managed to lose most of our house keys. Martin would be last to leave each morning, and he had mislaid both back door keys and his front door key. I was desperately trying to guard my key, until I had no option but to surrender it. We made an arrangement that, as he was the last to leave the house in the mornings, he would lock up and leave the key under a certain plant pot. Did he remember to do that? No! On days that Mick was working with him, I would come home, lift the appropriate plant pot, lift up all the surrounding plant pots, and come to the conclusion that I was locked out! Sigh of exasperation! However, there was a silver lining to this scenario; it meant I got to spend time with old Annie.

Old Annie lived in the house next door. She was a widow and had her cat for company. She hadn't been able to have children, but had an attentive niece who kept an eye on her. She was always pleased to see me. Her house seemed frozen in time: there was always a pan of offal simmering on the stove, filling the house with its meaty aroma. It was a treat for her beloved cat who seemed to be permanently curled up asleep in a cut-glass bowl that would have formerly been used for fruit or Christmas trifle. Annie would be sitting in front of her coal fire, her bare legs dappled red from the heat of the fire, thick stockings rolled down round her ankles. She would usually have half a china cup of cold tea perched precariously in its saucer on the arm of the fireside chair she always occupied. We would talk about days gone by, how she met her husband, how she used to get warts on her hands from the stalks of the daffodils she harvested when she was a young girl working in rural Lancashire. Sometimes we would sit in silence and just stare into the dancing flames of the fire, happy to be in each other's company. Then I would hear the engine of the pickup truck which would signal my time to leave. It had been a time to slow down, to accept what I couldn't change, and to spend time in the company of a wise, resilient lady.

Spring was approaching, lighter nights, new birth, the feeling of hope as the world emerged from Winter's grip. I was hopeful that maybe we'd have some good news soon. Was I imagining that the smell of Annie's cat's offal was just a little unbearable and faintly nauseating!?

One day in early Spring, I was back teaching, after the Easter break. I suddenly felt very unwell and had severe pains in my stomach. I sent a child with a message to the teacher next door to please keep a check on my class and went to investigate what was happening. I had lost some blood! Oh no! For a moment, I was like a rabbit caught in headlights. I would have to go home. This seems obvious now, but back then, as a teacher, I felt duty bound to stay with my class. However, this was looking serious, so I asked the head if I could go home as I was feeling poorly. I kept the details to a minimum. He granted my request and somehow I got myself to the train station. I was praying all the way!!

Realistically, I should have got a taxi, but I was trying to keep things as low key and normal as possible. Amazingly, a young man who lived a few doors down the road from us was on the train, in the same carriage! He had been in college doing exams and was coming home early. Thank you God! He walked down the road with me. I didn't divulge that I wasn't feeling well, but I was **so** glad he was there. He left me to go to his house, and I was able to let go of my pretend sunny disposition. I was feeling wretched and desperate. As I approached my house I saw a striped heap on the road. Oh no, it looked very much like the silhouette of a cat. "Please don't let it be Tigger" (our cat). As I got nearer, I could see it was just an oily rag. Grateful for small mercies I made my way inside. Fortunately we'd had more keys cut, so that was another timely mercy.

I phoned Claire, my mother-in-law, and got into bed. She came round and called the doctor. It was the same dismissive doctor who had been rather matter of fact, but this time, after examining me, he said he was going to call a gynaecologist for an emergency home visit. Wow, things were getting a bit too serious for my liking. Fear began to creep up my body with its icy fingers. The promise I'd been holding on to seemed to be fading fast. I was hanging on to this promise by my finger nails, but it seemed futile. "God, please let everything stabilise, please let everything calm down."

The gynaecologist arrived, he seemed to have hands as big as shovels, and he deftly used them to give me an internal examination!! Well, so much for things calming down! He announced a suspected ectopic pregnancy, and I was to go by ambulance for an emergency operation! An ectopic pregnancy is where the foetus is developing in the fallopian tube and is deemed life-threatening to the mother. Shock and confusion! Of course, I was very tearful. I was also pretty miffed with God. Why, after getting pregnant after so long, would He allow it to be in the wrong place? It seemed so unfair.

The neighbours saw me bundled into the ambulance in my dressing gown. How humiliating! 'The woman who can't conceive, and when she does, it's in the wrong place!' All those words I'd read last time just seemed to ring hollow now. My tears flowed uncontrollably and my eyes were hot with grief and disappointment.

I was wheeled into a waiting room before being assessed. The lady I sat next to was really kind. She didn't want to be intrusive, but asked if I was ok. I managed to tell her, through the sobs, that I had a suspected ectopic pregnancy. Amazingly, she said that she'd had one of those, but it hadn't stopped her from going on to raise a family. I was instantly comforted. I had to sheepishly thank God for His kindness in providing those words of reassurance through her.

I was prepped for my operation. I asked the surgeon if there was any chance of saving the baby, would they please do so. I drifted off into oblivion.

When I came round, I whispered a "thank you" to God that I was still alive! Martin was there at my bedside. I was so glad to see his face and hold his hand. The operation had been a success, however, it had not been for an ectopic pregnancy, but a burst ovarian cyst. That was sort of a relief. At least I hadn't lost a precious life. Once I was over this, we could try again. Maybe this is what had been causing all the problems.

My parents came over from Hull, and took me back there to convalesce for a few weeks. It was a treat to be looked after and have some rest and space to think. Maybe now, after this blip, things would get back on track…

There were a few more hurdles to overcome:

Firstly, somehow my body developed an intolerance to Martin's sperm, which is not good when trying to conceive! This resulted in another visit to the dear gynaecologist, who prescribed some cream which, presumably neutralised the pH and enabled us to resume normal relations. However, Martin's sperm was tested and it was discovered that he had a very low sperm count. This was a blow to us, but he made a joke about it and said he was like a Jaffa orange: "all fruit and no pips".

The thing to guard against when you are desperately trying to start a family, is allowing the mechanics to take over. Sometimes it can become all about conceiving and you forget about intimacy - the mind is focussed elsewhere. This was certainly happening with us, and it adds to the emotional exhaustion. There was also a barrage of well-meaning advice from various quarters, the suggestion to adopt (Martin was happily adopted), and just the fact that our private affairs now seemed to be in the public domain, added to my sense of failure, or our sense of failure, although Martin continued with his sunny disposition. My heart was aching for a child. I was on a constant emotional rollercoaster of "Will I fall pregnant this month? Could I be pregnant? No, not this time". I lost count of how many times I went over my due date, only to be disappointed a couple of weeks later.

On one occasion we were in Wales on a church weekend away. Martin and I were in a cafe on the Saturday morning. He was reading the newspaper - something he rarely got opportunity to do. There was a gorgeous blond-haired, blue-eyed baby boy gurgling in his carrier seat by his mother's chair. He was the image of my heart's desire. It was torment for me. I couldn't bear it any longer. I slid my chair back and exited the cafe at pace, running, running, running as far as I could go, my chest feeling like it would explode. I didn't know where I was running to, I just wanted to escape the constant cycle of disappointment. I could hear Martin's voice behind me, calling me to stop. I did eventually stop. I felt so foolish for running away, but I felt so wretched at being unable to control my destiny and plans. I began to grow disappointed with God. The serpent of cynicism was tightening around my heart. I was angry with Him, for promising me something and not delivering. I was even more disappointed that, not only was I not able to hold onto pregnancies, but, with Martin's poor sperm count, the odds of conceiving were further reduced. Why was this so difficult? Why was God withholding my heart's desire?

The frustrating thing about being angry with God is that it's a no win situation. It's 'cutting off your nose to spite your face', as the saying goes. He's the source of all love, peace, comfort and grace. He's the author of life itself, so it's pretty stupid to fall out with Him! Of course, He continues to love us and patiently wait for us to come back to Him. He's not fazed by our tantrums, He welcomes our questions, He's a good and patient Father, but we cannot always understand His ways.

I began to realise this when I picked up my Bible again and started reading where I believe I was led to, so I would be encouraged once again. Firstly in Genesis, the first book of the Bible, where Abraham mildly complains to God that he hasn't any children, so all his inheritance will pass to his servant, Eliezer. God replies:

"Behold, the LORD'S word came to him, saying, "This man will not be your heir, but he who will come out of your own body will be your heir." (Genesis 15:4)

That phrase leapt out at me. It seemed very significant - another promise, or rather, an assurance that the promise had not been forgotten about, and I would conceive and have the desire of my heart. Shortly after that, I read about Abraham's wife, Sarah:

'..By faith even Sarah herself received power to conceive, and she bore a child when she was past age, since she counted him faithful who had promised. Therefore as many as the stars of the sky in multitude, and as innumerable as the sand which is by the sea shore, were fathered by one man, and him as good a dead." (Hebrews 11:11)

So, here's a mild rebuke and instruction for me: continue to have faith, and to trust that God is faithful, no matter what the circumstances look like. Apparently, Sarah was in her nineties when she conceived Isaac. I hoped I didn't have to wait that long! And as for poor Abraham, rather unkindly described, it was to show that God often waits until things are impossible before He creates a miracle.

Fresh faith rose up in me. God had spoken positively to me. It was like a new page had begun, and I reaffirmed my trust in Him and told Him I was sorry for doubting Him. And although I fully admire those who choose the children they love through adoption, as with Martin and his siblings, I believed that I would conceive and birth a child.

Chapter Four

Faith Being Tested!

So with new hope we continued with our lives and shared some wonderful adventures together: we travelled to Zimbabwe where Martin and some other builders from across the UK converted the buildings of an old tobacco farm into a Bible school. I went along for part of the time armed with a suitcase of wool and knitting needles. At crack of dawn, the day after I arrived, I had a queue of ladies at my door waiting to relieve me of my bounty. I (patronisingly) asked them if they wanted me to teach them how to knit. Clearly not, as they came to see me over the coming days with beautifully cabled hats and garments they'd knitted for their babies - without a pattern! They had knitted throughout the night by candlelight, such was their glee at receiving the treasure of wool and knitting needles!

We returned from that beautiful country with lots of stories and an appreciation of how materially rich we were, although the joy, contentment and generosity of the people we met was very humbling.

It had been good to focus on just living life and not being consumed by the desire of my heart. I was able to leave it 'in God's hands' which lifted a burden off us both.

Back home there were a couple of ladies with whom I met regularly to pray. Their names were Viv and Pat. On one occasion, Viv had sensed God say that something significant would happen in November. I put that thought on the back burner, I didn't want to cling too tightly to any specifics, I would wait and see.

I was continuing to teach full time at a Junior school in Liverpool. It was an early start each day, catching the train and a bus, running a home, being involved with church activities (we were very much involved with the youth work). I was beginning to feel very tired. I also became aware that all was not well physically as I suffered terrible stinging when I went to the toilet. I decided to make an appointment with the doctor.

His diagnosis sent me reeling - genital herpes! How on earth....!?

Martin came to pick me up from the doctor's surgery. I told him what the doctor had said. He could see the disbelief and puzzlement in my face. How could I have a sexually transmitted disease? He assured me he'd been faithful to me, and I told him I believed him, I had no reason to doubt him. I reassured him of my fidelity too. We hugged and I cried. Another challenge to face, which entailed visits to the STD clinic in Southport. I signed off school sick, because the blisters were so painful, I could not bear to sit down. I had to sit on an inflatable ring. I was just too embarrassed to divulge to my Headmaster why I was on sick leave.

Sitting in the waiting room at the STD clinic was very humbling. It was the time when AIDS had come to light and there was a great sense of stigma and shame connected to it. There were posters about it on the walls. Although I was firmly convinced that this outbreak in my body must have a completely innocent explanation, I couldn't help feeling that people might be judging me or Martin. People who know nothing about us. It was quite sobering to think how often we do that - make judgments and assumptions about people when we have few, if any, facts on which to base our opinions. And indeed, they are only opinions.

The team who dealt with my case were wonderful. They were kind, caring and non-judgmental. I would need a few visits, and I was given medication. I had a counsellor who explained that I would always have the virus in my body; it could flare up at any time, especially during periods of stress. It could also be passed on to any children I might conceive, especially if I had an outbreak during delivery. This was all very disconcerting news. Here was another complication to deal with. It was like a sword of Damocles hanging over my head. An imminent and ever-present peril. I decided I would break my silence and invite my church leaders to come and pray for me.

There are clear instructions in the Bible about what to do if you are ill or suffering physically in any way.

*"Is anyone among you sick? Let him call for the elders of the assembly *(church), and let them pray over him, anointing him with oil in the name of the Lord; and the prayer of faith will heal him who is sick, and the Lord will raise him up. If he has committed sins, he will be forgiven."* (James 5:14-15).

*my addition. Of course this promise is not just for males only, but generic for humanity.

This was common practice in our church so, even though it was excruciatingly embarrassing, I invited Dave, Jim and David over to pray for me. Jim, as he was praying, sensed a fire burning up the virus. I didn't feel any different. I continued with the medication and eventually returned to work and life. However, as I will refer to later, something extremely significant happened that day.

As I was back at school sitting at my desk, I noticed that at least six children in my class had active cold sores. In fact there was nothing recent or unusual in that. There was the answer to my puzzle! Marking books, sharpening pencils, performing the everyday tasks of a teacher, I had picked up the virus on my fingers and the rest was history. If only hand gel had been more widely available then!

I had to take stock of what had happened. The Bible teaches that we have an adversary, and he's only really bothered about harassing us if we are causing him problems by being active in our faith. So, if you are facing difficulties, it could be a back-handed compliment that you are actually doing well. Of course, Christians believe that Jesus has overcome **all** the power of the enemy when he died on the Cross and rose again three days later. That's something we need to keep reminding ourselves of when we are ambushed by problems. I had to grasp hold of my newly downloaded refreshed faith and find reasons to be thankful. First of all, for a loving, caring husband and a network of supportive people around me, for free healthcare and people who had researched and created medications and treatments.

We were now coming into early Spring 1988. I love that season of freshness and new life everywhere. I was beginning to feel the stirrings of new life in my own body. Could I dare hope that this was finally happening to me? I decided I needed to wait a little longer before doing anything to confirm things. February, March, April passed, so I decided to make an appointment to see a doctor. I wasn't able to see my usual doctor, but another doctor in the practice, who was usually booked up because he was so popular with patients. He listened to me, examined me, asked me a few questions. This was good. I wasn't being dismissed as being neurotic. He then told me there was definitely some enlargement of my womb, but I wasn't as far advanced as my dates suggested. He arranged for me to go for a scan at the hospital. Although there was need for caution, I was excited that I seemed to have made some tiny steps of progress. I was being taken seriously. I broke the news to Martin. It was not yet time to break open the champagne, but there was hope.

I was admitted to a day ward. Unbelievably there were women there waiting for abortions, alongside those with threatened miscarriages. Women with completely different emotional needs lumped together in a small space. For me, there was so much hanging on the outcome of this scan, I could hardly speak. I'm usually quite friendly and try to find something to converse about, but this was hard. I eventually established that the lady next to me was on bed rest and clinging on to her baby by her fingernails. I realised there were other women in the same plight as me. Not everybody fell pregnant at the drop of a hat. It was not a subject that was talked about much in those days. There was a strange comfort in meeting other women who could understand the heartache.

I was required to drink a large jug of water, and in due course I would be taken for my scan. I waited... and waited.. and waited... I was absolutely bursting for a wee. I called for a nurse and was reassured they wouldn't be long. Time passed and I could wait no longer. I went to the bathroom. I had a pain in my stomach, and much more than wee splurged into the toilet. I had a download of understanding in my head about what had just happened. My baby had died inside me however long ago, and now I had just passed it. I sat there for a while. I didn't cry. I uttered a silent prayer for my lost one. I committed his or her little spirit to God. I just wanted to be at home now and be quiet.

I got back to my bed and managed to flag a clearly overworked nurse to tell her what had happened. I told her I'd like to telephone my husband to come and collect me, (there were no mobile phones in those days, except for high flying entrepreneurs). I didn't want examining or discussing. There was nothing to be done and I just wanted the sanctuary of being at home. Amazingly, she complied with my wishes and Martin duly came to collect me.

That evening the local churches were holding a joint meeting of prayer and praise. I told Martin that I wanted to go, so we did. Being in the presence of people worshipping God was so comforting to me. A warm assurance began to fill my heart, and I felt a consolation that I had gone further than before with a pregnancy. I realised that I was not alone in my plight and this dear doctor had believed me. There was hope.

I went back to see him the following week. He was on my case! He had noticed that my blood group is Rhesus negative, and so arranged for me to go for an Anti-D injection. This is to prevent a woman's body from producing antibodies that would attack a Rhesus positive foetus in the womb, thinking it was a foreign body. That's what had been happening to my babies. Martin was Rhesus positive.

He also discussed with me the prospect of a procedure called GIFT (gamete intrafallopian transfer). This is where a woman's eggs are removed and combined with healthy sperm, then introduced back into the fallopian tube for fertilisation to take place.

Yesss! We were getting some answers to those things which had puzzled us for so long! My mission now was to make sure that Martin was producing healthy sperm. I researched and found that wearing loose boxer shorts, and eating certain foods all help to improve the quality of those little life-carriers, the former keeping things cool, the latter providing the necessary nutrients.

One evening I came in from work and Martin was lolling on the couch.

"I've been thinking", he said, "what if you were to leave work? Maybe that would help your body to rest, which would help things?"

Those words were music to my ears. I leapt on him and kissed and thanked him profusely. Could we afford it? My salary was our regular income which paid the mortgage. His income was irregular due to him being self-employed and often suffering cash flow issues. He said we would trust God and find a way. So, I handed my notice in at school, to finish at the end of the Summer term.

Chapter Five

When A Plan Comes Together...

So July 1988 saw me having my final day at school. I'd loved teaching, and had especially enjoyed the humour of little Scousers. It amused me how their allegiance to whichever football team they supported coloured their whole view on life - and I mean coloured, literally. Those who supported Liverpool FC would have nothing blue in their possession, and likewise, Everton supporters would protest greatly if they were given anything red. I had to choose colours of exercise books carefully so I didn't cause unnecessary ructions.

I was tired though, and maybe this break would help my body prepare for motherhood, especially as now the medical picture was clearer and more hopeful. I think too that Martin was feeling more ready to start a family now. It was easy for me to forget that he was three years younger than me, only just 20 when we married in 1983.

We came across a Government scheme which would enable me to have a grant for doing my own work. I had to sign up on a weekly basis at the Employment Agency, and declare that I was willing to undertake employment, then after six months I would be eligible for payments. Great! I would sign on in September, as my teacher's pay covered us until the end of August. And, I would be employed as Martin's secretary, typing out estimates and invoices. I enrolled on a typing course at the local high school - this was before the days of laptops and word processors. It was much trickier than I expected, but I did enjoy the satisfying "ping" at the end of each line of type.

The months passed by and I was really enjoying the freedom of my new role. I was able to meet up with other people during the week, get on with personal projects, look after the domestic side of life more thoroughly, as well as keeping things going with Martin's administration and clerical work.

We decided, with our change of circumstances, that we should sort out our insurance policies. We gave the business to a young man who was just starting out with his company. He was the son of a friend. As part of the procedure Martin had to go for a medical. This brought up some shocking news..

We were lying in bed when Martin broke the news to me.

"The doc said I have an irregular heart beat. Nothing to be worried about now... probably need an operation in a few years' time.."

Telling me there was nothing to be worried about was like telling an ice lolly not to melt in the sun. Of course I was worried. There were so many 'What-ifs'.

Then, to make matters worse, Martin came out with, "Anyway, if anything happens to me, which it won't, I want you to marry again".

I was really cross with him. How could I ever even think of marrying someone else?! It was like an insult that I should even give it a millisecond of my thoughts. There's nobody else in the world that I would ever want to marry.

Poor guy, he got a tirade, but eventually I calmed down and was placated. It was something I could put out of my sleepy head. For now. It was much further down the line, decades, hopefully! We had a principle we lived by, that we would not go to sleep without resolving any issues that had cropped up. I realised he was thinking ahead to make sure I would be happy in the worst-case scenario.

"Be a rucksack!" That was his usual invitation to me to snuggle up against his back before we fell asleep. Tomorrow was a new day.

During these months of signing on at the Employment Agency, a lady from church had been trying to persuade me to do some supply work at the school where she worked. Doreen was School Secretary at a primary school on a very needy housing estate on the edge of Liverpool. She spoke with a broad Yorkshire accent and was always immaculately dressed. Her husband was a bank manager. He too had a dapper dress code. She was not the sort of person you say "No" to.

I would try and dodge her at church meetings but, every week she would pursue me, telling me how desperate they were for a supply teacher. Every week I would hold out, simperingly saying that I was so close to completing my six months of signing on, that it would be foolish.... With just a week to go, I relented and agreed to do some supply work at her school. I was cross with myself, but Doreen's Yorkshire grit and determination was overpowering. I went to visit the school.

The Headmistress was a lovely lady called Brenda. She looked like she was nearing retirement, although she was very jolly and colourful, with amazing hair styled like a chrysanthemum.

I needed a car to get to my new job. Amazingly, someone at church was selling one cheaply, so I took possession of a little red Ford Fiesta.

I worked full time at that school for the last half of the Spring term. It was the hardest place I'd ever worked. At the end of each day I would be so physically and emotionally exhausted, I would have to sit quietly for fifteen minutes in my little red car just to get things together in my brain. Playground duty was a nightmare - breaking up fights the whole time. Trying to maintain peace and order in the classroom was to be congratulated. Actually managing to teach anything was commendable. Many of these children came from a culture of theft in order to sustain drug abuse habits, insecure family dynamics and poverty. There was a permanent job coming up, and I was asked if I would like to apply. Really? I take my hat off to all the amazing staff who worked in that place, they were a great and dedicated bunch of people, but I would definitely not want to join their ranks on a permanent basis. It was far too stressful, and I was supposed to be winding down. It was like I had jumped out of the frying pan and into the fire. The school was constantly being broken into and vandalised, another event to which staff had become accustomed. What is telling though, is that I don't remember a single child from that school, they are erased from my memory, yet I can remember children, and even their names, from all the other places I taught at.

The Head very generously told me of a Catholic Primary school up the road from them. She said that they might be looking for a part-time teacher after Easter. I went along to meet the Headmaster and visit the school. It was a haven. Although open plan, there was a calm - a lovely hum of children engaged in their tasks. It was hard to believe it was the same catchment area.

I got the job and started working there three days a week after the Easter holidays. It meant I was still able to do Martin's clerical work on the other two days without needing to rely on Government payments. I really enjoyed being back in the classroom especially in such a lovely, happy environment. There were still issues, many children came from homes which struggled with poverty, but there was a much stronger sense of hope, love and community.

Chapter Six

...And Then It Goes Pear-Shaped

It was a dark, stormy October evening. I had been to my usual Monday evening prayer meeting; Viv, Pat and myself would meet to chat and pray about issues in our lives that concerned us. We'd recently gained a new member, Adrienne. Just as we were winding things up, Adrienne said she'd had a visual image of me, (I felt excited, maybe I was cradling a child?) She saw me climbing out of a boat and walking on the water towards Jesus. (This alludes to the Bible story of Peter walking on the stormy sea to affirm his trust in Jesus: (Matthew 14:22-36; Mark 6:45-56; John 6:16-24).

I felt disturbed and very puzzled. This was not what I wanted to hear. I'd had enough setbacks! An ominous chill swept over me and dread filled the pit of my stomach. I was secretly cross with Adrienne for telling me this, and I tried to make light of it, but I was deeply troubled. As I got into my car, the weather reflected my mood: swirling winds scattering the Autumn leaves, pelting rain splattered on the windscreen, which the whirring wipers worked hard to clear; their frenzied motion made it hard to focus on the road ahead. At one stage of my journey home I was conscious that a hubcap had come off a rear wheel, and I had to stop the car to retrieve it.

It was a relief to get home. It was around 10-00pm. Unusually, Martin was already in bed. He'd been feeling nauseous and had a bad headache. Adrienne's final words crept back into my thoughts, but I wouldn't verbalise them. I climbed into bed beside him. Subdued and distracted with fear and anxiety, we exchanged thoughts about it being some sort of virus, having a good night's sleep and tomorrow being a new day. A kiss goodnight, lights out! But that picture of the solitary figure climbing out of the boat and falteringly reaching towards Jesus kept on lapping over me like the stormy waves crashing over rocks.. Questions! Why was it just me in the boat? I was focussing on the solitary figure. Like Peter, I was looking at the swirling water, I was not seeing the outstretched arms of Jesus reaching out to grab me. It was too much to think about. Too painful to think about, surely God still had to fulfil his promise of a child, so it would all be ok, Adrienne must have made a mistake. Sleep eventually overcame my thoughts.

Tuesday morning saw Martin getting up and dressed ready for a day's work. He wasn't as chipper and cheerful as usual, and I suggested in vain that he took it easy and rested for the day. No! People were expecting him, schedules needed keeping to. I understood that; as a self-employed builder he wasn't entitled to sick pay, and time was money, and most importantly for Martin, he couldn't let people down. He said he would be alright, and no, he didn't have time to see the doctor, it had just been a virus. Normality resumed and we got through our day without any eventualities.

Wednesday came. I only worked mornings on Wednesdays, so I was home in the afternoon. I received a phone call from Nina, a friend from church. She and her husband usually hosted a weekly small group meeting at their house, but they were decorating the lounge and wondered if we could host instead. That was fine. I had time to tidy up and make sure there was enough biscuits and milk for hot drinks.

Martin came home unexpectedly early in the afternoon. I thought he looked grey and drawn. His usually sunny disposition was overshadowed by a pained expression from a bad headache, according to him, nothing that a cup of tea and couple of biscuits wouldn't cure - his go-to remedy for most things. I told him we were hosting the home group meeting and he said he had a couple of potential customers to visit after our evening meal, then he would join us later. Once again, his can-do, push-through mentality kicked in; a bit of a headache wasn't going to stop him, but I was getting worried. He would usually be singing, humming or joking, but he seemed subdued and serious.

Maybe he could see that I was looking anxious. We were having (yet another) cup of tea after our evening meal before he went to visit customers to price up jobs.

" Are you okay?" he asked me.

"Yes", I shrugged, "Why?" (I hadn't told him about Monday's 'picture').

"You don't seem yourself".

Why was he saying this? In a split second my brain rattled through what his comment could mean:

'You're letting yourself go',

'You're looking older',

'You're not making the most of your appearance'.

I could have retorted a defensive reply or flipped the remark to focus on him, or just gone into withdrawn, sulky silent mode, but thankfully I didn't. Something stopped me and I simply remarked that I had been feeling a bit tired,

Tea supped, a quick peck on the cheek and he was off and out to see his clients. I got final things done before people started arriving.

We were just chatting, drinking tea and catching up with people's weekly news when Martin returned home about 8pm. He popped his head round the door and greeted everyone, announced he was going for a quick bath and would join us later. We carried on with our meeting. About an hour had passed, I cleared the cups onto a tray and carried them out to the kitchen. The unfolding events must have happened very quickly but felt like they were in slow motion. I heard a strange noise, like someone sawing wood. I stopped and tried to discern where it was coming from - upstairs! Martin had been a long time. Suddenly it hit me like a bolt out the blue. I ran up the stairs several at a time. The bathroom door was locked! There was no answer from him to my calls, but the rasping noise was definitely from there. It was his laboured breathing. I am only a petite build, but I kicked the door open like a ninja warrior.

Martin was lying on the floor in his bathrobe, his face was pale and his lips were blue and he was unconscious, a quick look confirmed he hadn't even got into the bath , which was full, but the taps were off. Thank God for that! He might have drowned.

I screamed downstairs for help, my head felt anaesthetised and everything seemed heavy as lead.

This was me alone in the boat!

This was time to walk on the water!

We got Martin in the recovery position and I kept trying to talk to him, but I was shaking like a leaf and in shock myself. The paramedics arrived quickly and soon had the situation under control. Someone made sure that both sets of parents were informed and a whole load of people asked to start praying. Laurie and Claire (Martin's parents), arrived to drive me to the hospital after the ambulance had left. As we were closing the front door getting ready to leave, the police arrived and a plain clothed officer requested to search the house. A boldness came over me, I was annoyed that he was delaying me. This was an emergency!

"What for?", I snapped.

"In case there are any substances, Madam".

"You'll be lucky to find as much as a paracetamol", I told him and got into the car. As far as I know he abandoned the search.

I suppose, given Martin's age, he wanted to make sure there were no suspicious circumstances, drugs or violence.

I watched the flashing blue light disappear down the road ahead of us. Adrenalin was kicking in, my heart was racing and my hands were cold and clammy. I was feeling horribly helpless.

"Oh God, please let this just be a dream!"

We arrived at Fazakerley Hospital and met with my church leaders. The staff let us take over a waiting room to pray. There was a wonderful network of people who offered support and joined the prayer vigil that had started for Martin in their homes. There was no social media then, so communicating things was by landline. Hardly anyone had mobile phones.

I was required to answer a lot of questions so the staff could build a picture as to what had happened. The medical team was busy working on him to get him stabilised. It was surreal waiting in that room. There was no conversation to be had, at least not from me. I just wanted to wake up from this nightmare. I repeated over and over, "Oh God, please don't let him die."

Eventually, a doctor summoned myself and Laurie and Claire to update us. They had managed to get Martin stable, he'd had a big bleed to his brain, probably triggered by the virus. We couldn't see him now, but everything possible was being done to keep him comfortable. We were encouraged to go home and get some rest - there was nothing we could do. We were told they would know more in the morning, and were hopeful there could be an operation with a 70% chance of recovery.

"What could that mean?", I thought. At least I would still have my lovely Martin.

I went back to Laurie and Claire's house for the night. My eyes were as heavy as lead; sleep refused to come. I could hear Martin's mum sobbing in her bedroom. I was thankful for the people who I knew would be praying through the night, but the dread of what tomorrow might bring felt like icy fingers running down my spine. I shivered in the straight jacket of the single bed and waited for the light of dawn, whispering my prayers into the silence.

This was me in the boat on my own.

We got through the night! It was Thursday. I reminisced the events of the previous day. Thank goodness the group meeting had been changed to our house. I would have come home to face that trauma all alone. Martin would almost certainly have been dead and I would have been too late to speak to him ever again. It was indeed a mercy that I'd been surrounded by others who were able to support us. I was grateful. Actually, I was not alone!

We phoned the hospital for a progress report. The medical team had managed to keep him stable through the night and were planning to move him to Walton hospital, which specialised in neurology; there he would have further tests and a possible operation. That seemed like encouraging news. I snatched hold of my ray of hope!

I went home to change my clothes and get ready to visit Martin in the hospital. I remembered our last conversation. I was so glad that I hadn't been moody or caused an argument. As I looked in the mirror at my piggy eyes after a sleepless night, I did my best with eyeshadow and mascara; I wanted him to know that I had heard him and was making an effort.

My parents had travelled to my house from Hull after receiving the news, so we went to the hospital together. The news on our arrival was not good. Martin had deteriorated during the journey between hospitals and was now on a life support machine. The medical team said there was no response from him, but he could probably still hear. I was allowed to go in and see him.

"I'll get a response from him", I determined, and made my way into the cubicle. This was the first time I'd seen him since the awful events of

Wednesday evening. His colour was restored and his breathing deep and rhythmic: he looked like he was in a deep and restful sleep - I had to remind myself that it was a machine doing the work. I stroked his arm and kissed him on the forehead.

"Hello, my Love." I said. "Look at you with all these lovely nurses looking after you!"

My throat tightened as I realised how poorly he was. It would take a miracle to restore him. It was hard to see this usually cheerful, mischievous man of mine laid out like a sleeping prince. If only I could wake him with a kiss.

I came away. By this time the waiting area was full of friends and relatives who had come to visit Martin, including two of our church pastors. They were expectant that prayer for healing would turn the situation around: I was hoping they were right. We all spoke in hushed tones. It was that 'walking on egg shells' feeling when you're trying to avoid breaking something precious or waking a sleeping giant. There were plenty of funny stories to remember about Martin, and it was a comfort that everyone was trying to think of cheery things to say, but the elephant was in the room and it wasn't going away! One visitor could be heard making his way down the corridor whistling a merry tune. Rather inappropriate, you might think. It was a man from church and school who I called Blackbird Jones because of his whistling prowess. He himself had suffered difficulties and sadness in his life: his toddler son had drowned in the garden pond, and his wife had died of cancer. His love for Jesus, however, meant that he was always full of joy. He had recently remarried a retired school teacher called Margaret, finding love in later life.

I did not want to leave the hospital, but having had very little sleep the previous night, I was feeling pretty ropey. The wonderful staff turned a side room into a place where I could lie down and have a nap.

I wasn't really expecting to sleep, but it was lovely to lie down in a quiet place and close my eyes knowing there was a dedicated team looking after Martin and keeping him comfortable.

As I dozed, a picture came into my mind. In my imagination I could clearly see a chrysalis hanging from a branch. Its body casing began to split open; I watched as a crumpled butterfly wriggled itself out of its imprisoning casing. Its beautiful wings began expanding, and when they were fully formed it took flight. Free at last, it joyfully ascended into its destiny.

Then, in my thoughts I sensed an explanation being downloaded: the chrysalis was Martin. His spirit was wriggling free from his mortal body. Would it be kind to crumple that butterfly and try to stuff it back into the casing again? No! That butterfly: Martin, had to be allowed to be free.

As believers in Christ and his promise of resurrection life, I knew that this freedom was also eternal safety. Even if Martin were to have an operation, (which was looking less likely now), he might not recover all his faculties. I would be there as his carer, of course, but how would he cope with disability? I know of and admire people who have recovered from brain injury, and their devoted carers have been given grace and strength to look after them, but I believed God was telling me it was Martin's time to be released from this earth. It would be a kindness to let him go.

I went back into the waiting room full of family and friends. Silently I sat down and with my head cupped in my hands, I cried out the words of Jesus as He faced the prospect of His crucifixion in the Garden of Gethsemane (see Matthew 26:39):

"Oh God, if it's possible, let this cup pass from me. But let Your will be done, not mine". (My paraphrase).

Gethsemane was an olive grove - a place where olives were picked and crushed to release their oil. I was not facing anything like the agonies which Jesus was facing: flogging, crucifixion, bearing the sins of the whole world; but I was feeling crushed; God had shown me it was time to let go, to say goodbye, but it was so hard, so painful. However, counter-intuitively, it would be my final act of love.

I related the images and impressions I'd received to those in the waiting room. I told my church leaders that in the light of what I'd just experienced, I didn't think it was appropriate to pray for Martin; it wasn't lack of faith, but a response to what I had seen so clearly: it would be a mercy. I could hardly believe the words I was saying, but I felt an inner strength that wasn't my own. It was the hardest thing, but it was right.

The medical team were so amazingly attentive to Martin's needs, washing him down and constantly monitoring him. There was a calm there; it seemed like we could have stayed like that indefinitely. The consultant said they would do a brain scan in the morning to see if there was any activity, but I knew what God had shown me: Martin's spirit was wriggling out of its chrysalis and pumping its wings with blood for the homeward flight. God had prepared me, just as He'd done on Monday night. His warning was a kindness, not a curse.

We all went home and that evening I updated those who might want to come and say their final farewells.

Friday morning came and I returned to the hospital with both sets of parents. Laurie, Claire and myself had a meeting with the consultant; a kind, portly man who had the demeanour of a benevolent uncle. He explained that the scans had confirmed that there was no brain activity whatsoever. It was highly likely that the virus of Monday evening had triggered a massive brain haemorrhage, nothing more could be done. I could tell that he was gearing up to breaking the difficult news of what these findings meant next. I was so grateful that God had given me prior warning through the butterfly picture. I took a deep breath, conscious of poor Claire, I uttered the words;

" It's alright, I know you will need to switch the machine off soon, but I know Martin's spirit has left his body already. Please could you give us time? There are some people travelling over to say their last goodbyes. I really appreciate everything you and your team has done."

He seemed taken aback, but relieved at the response. Martin's mum buckled and sobbed deeply; that was hard to witness. I had pronounced something so final, but I believe it was the right thing. If there had been the minutest chance that Martin could recover, I would have grasped it in a heartbeat. God had shown me something; science had confirmed it.

With composure that came from somewhere deep, I gave Martin's forehead a final kiss and thanked him for the wonderful decade we'd shared together. If he could still hear, I didn't want him to know how broken I was feeling. Then I invited those in the waiting area to to say their final farewells.

Chapter Seven

Farewell But Not Goodbye

Finally, in the solitude of my bedroom, was I able to let the raging torrent of grief flow freely. My new reality kicked in - I was a widow, and the pain of it was like a throbbing stab wound. I felt as though half of me had been amputated. Was it only three days ago? It seemed like a lifetime! My whole life had tumbled like a house of cards. He was safe, I was sure of that; on the back-burner of my mind I rejoiced that he was enjoying the glorious things that God has prepared for those who love Him (see 1 Corinthians 2:9); but I was left behind, and it hurt so much. Nothing would be the same again.

"Why God? Why did you have to take him so soon? What about Your promise of a family? Does this serve any purpose at all? I don't understand why this has happened to me."

After crying my tear ducts dry, I tried to clear away reminders that Martin was gone: shoes left in the hall, clothes strewn on the bathroom floor. It took a while because every few minutes I would be hit by another tsunami of grief as I hugged and smelled his clothes. It was exhausting.

I determined to go to church on Sunday. I was able to be brave, I spoke of Martin as a Peter Pan sort of person: he was taken in his prime, he wouldn't ever grow old like the rest of us! We would be reunited with him again. In terms of the whole of eternity,18 years or 80 doesn't make much difference! Yes, I was able to be brave for a short while, then floored again, and hardly able to stand up.

The days leading up to the funeral were filled with people bringing cards, flowers, food. They had kind words to say, and funny stories; sometimes there were awkward silences as we realised how much we were missing him already. I realised that it had been a terrible shock for them too. Martin was only 26, yet he'd shared his short life with so many people, touched them with his fun, kindness and generosity. We were all trying to support each other as we reeled from the suddenness of this tragedy. But they would go home to their relatively normal lives. My reality had changed forever. All the colours had been washed off the canvas of my life, and now there were only greys. Sometimes, people would talk of normal, mundane things, such as the colour they were going to paint their lounge, or the bargain they'd just bought from the fashion outlet. I don't mean to be rude, but, I didn't care! What did it even matter? I felt alienated from normal life.

The worst visit was from the undertaker. I couldn't believe it when he produced a pile of glossy catalogues of coffins to choose from; it made me feel quite queasy. I was shocked at the commercialisation of death. I knew Martin wouldn't be bothered with a flashy casket, so I opted for the basic model. After the funeral director had left, I couldn't help a wry smile, thinking back to Martin's days as a grave digger and some of the amusing things that happened to him: Once, he was still by the grave in his muddy attire as the funeral party were arriving. Out of respect, he knew he had to get out of sight. He slid down a coal shoot into the church crypt, but then of course he couldn't get back out again. No mobile phones! He had to wait until the ceremony was over, and then yell and yell until eventually someone heard him and alerted a key holder to come to his rescue.

It may have surprised many people, but one of Martin's favourite canticles was the Nunc dimittis or Song of Simeon. We used to hear it recited when we attended the evening service at the church where he dug the graves (this attendance was part of the conditions of our rental agreement). It is found in Luke 2: 29-32, and is the praise response of Simeon, the aged priest, when the infant Jesus was presented at the temple. This was to fulfil the rite of purification according to Jewish custom:

" Now you are releasing your servant, Master, according to your word, in peace; for my eyes have seen your salvation, which you have prepared before the face of all peoples; a light for revelation to the nations, and the glory of your people Israel."

I thought it would be a lovely item to include in the funeral service. I asked the worship band from our church if they could sing it. They composed an amazing a cappella version. The funeral was to take place in the church which Martin's parents attended, which was just a couple of hundred yards down the road from our house. The evening before the funeral, some family members and I went down to church to check on final arrangements. The group were practising the Nunc dimittis. Oh my goodness! It was so beautiful, I buckled with emotion. What a good job I'd heard that before the day of the funeral. I now would be able to brace myself. What a lovely tribute to Martin. He was truly able to depart in peace.

Friday morning's weather reflected the sombreness of the occasion - grey skies and drizzling rain. I hadn't needed a funeral car because of living so near to the church. The hearse carrying Martin arrived and we all duly got ourselves in place behind it. Big strong blokes bearing the coffin on their shoulders, fighting back the tears in their final act of service to him. As I stood behind the coffin waiting to process up the path leading into the church, a sudden panic hit my stomach. Looking sideways up the extending, straight, aptly named Long Lane, the thought came to me that I could kick off my heels and just run, run, run. It was that same feeling I had in the Welsh cafe, all those years ago. But of course I knew I couldn't. I looked up at the flower-strewn coffin; some words Martin once said came into my mind: "You can't put God in a box!" No, and you can't put a child of His in a box! Courage came back to me with those words, like a warmth streaming through my veins. No, I knew Martin, the essence of him, was not in that box; his physical remains were, but not his spirit. He was safe and at peace. This was our opportunity to celebrate him and give him a rousing send off. The procession began, and with renewed composure I joined the many hearts who knew and loved Martin, and had come to say farewell. There were over 200 people packed into that church, from all sorts of backgrounds: family, friends, builder colleagues, school friends, people Martin had rubbed shoulders with throughout his life. I hoped they enjoyed the uplifting singing and comforting words that were offered. It was important, and I knew Martin would agree, that everyone had the opportunity to hear that there's more to this life than just this life. Those of us who believe the claims of Jesus have a sure hope that this was only "so long" and not "goodbye", even though parting is so difficult and painful.

There was another funeral straight after Martin's. It was of a young firefighter, and there were many people starting to arrive to support his family. As we were gathered around Martin's grave, I started singing an old hymn which was popular at the time:

"Turn you eyes upon Jesus,

Look full in His wonderful face,

And the things of earth will grow strangely dim

In the light of His glory and grace."

(Helen H. Lemmel (1922) public domain.)

Those who knew it joined in. It was a poignant reminder that when we are lost and don't know how to carry on, He gives us hope and reassurance.

Chapter Eight

Questions and Answers

The day after the funeral I came down to earth with a bump. The planning had kept me occupied, but now I had to come to terms with my new normal. I had plenty of supportive friends and family around me, but they had to get back to their normal lives too, and sometimes the kindness could be overkill when I just wanted times of solitude to grieve and let my tears flow without making anybody feel awkward.

It was late October, a poignant time of year. Martin and I used to enjoy bird watching, and this was the time when skeins of geese would come flying in to overwinter at Martin Mere wildlife reserve. We would often pack up sandwiches and trek out to watch them. The sandwiches had usually been eaten before we even arrived at the bird reserve! The geese were beginning to fly over now, and every time I heard their honking, or looked up to see their V formation, it would bring back so many memories. Martin's mum wrote a poem:

As the long-necked geese were flying

And the leaves were turned to gold,

God called you gently to Him -

Keeps you safe within His fold.

How wonderful to know you,

Through the years of growing up,

To lose you now in manhood

Is a very bitter cup.

Yet each and every memory

Is ours to cherish yet,

And as the years unroll ahead

We never will forget.

As the long-necked geese go flying

And the leaves are turned to gold,

We will remember Martin -

Always young, and never old.

(Claire Hughes 1989)

Yes, all I had now were memories, photographs, stories. The finality of my situation was so raw and painful; I knew I was in a precarious position. I had choices to make: I could slide down into a deep depression of sadness and morbidity, or I could try and be stoical and push through. In reality, I felt like a wilted lettuce leaf, but I wanted to make sense of what had happened, I wanted some answers: I needed to really get to grips with reading my Bible.

At bedtime I would be quite nervous, finding myself needing to investigate every creak and bump. I would check that I'd locked the doors several times, and even look in cupboards for hidden dangers. It was quite exhausting! I started to read Psalm 91.

"1 He who dwells in the secret place of the Most High will rest in the shadow of the Almighty. 2 I will say of the LORD, " He is my refuge and my fortress; my God, in whom I trust." 3 For He will deliver you from the snare of the fowler, and from the deadly pestilence. 4 He will cover you with His feathers Under his wings you will take refuge."

The whole psalm was about God watching over us and keeping us safe from every eventuality. We are safely hidden in His secret, impenetrable pavilion and He wraps His magnificent, protective wings round us, like an eagle shielding its young from danger. I would read it every night before I went to sleep, and would sense the peace and comfort of the words lapping over me and washing anxiety away.

Another surprising passage I felt led to, which I'd never noticed before, was in Deuteronomy 34:7-8. It concerned the death of the great Patriarch, Moses; the man who had delivered God's people from slavery in Egypt and sojourned with them for forty years through the wilderness, guiding them through the Red Sea, performing miracles, bringing them the Ten Commandments - a major figure in their history.

It said that the people mourned him for **thirty days.**

That was astonishing! Hardly any time at all for someone so pivotal. It seemed so inadequate! I felt like I would grieve for Martin forever, that my heart would always be like an empty gift box that had lost its treasure. I pondered, maybe the people of that particular culture grieved differently from the stiff-upper lipped British? Maybe they had a corporate, more abandoned outpouring, which would be too exhausting to maintain for any longer? Thirty days!

I came across other passages too, which seemed to leap off the page and grab my attention - words which were so pertinent to my situation. One was that the marriage covenant was valid only until death, and then the living partner was free to marry again (see 1 Corinthians 7:40, Romans 7:2). Indeed, they were encouraged to if they were a young widow (see 1 Timothy 5:14). Also, Jesus was quizzed by some Sadducees about the question of resurrection. He was asked whose wife a woman would be if she had been widowed several times and married successive brothers, as was the custom in Jewish Law. He replied that in the resurrection people will not marry or be married because they will be like the angels in heaven (see Matthew 22:30). The Book of Revelation speaks about Jesus (Christ) being the Bridegroom (Lamb), and the Church being His Bride (see chapter 19:7-9). Earthly marriage is a picture of the heavenly reality that is to come at the end of this age. Wow! This is so different from what many people believe. We have adopted a 'Hollywood' idea of marriage, love and romance.

If you are familiar with the movie 'Titanic', you will know that Rose meets Jack on the great ship and they fall in love. Tragedy strikes and Jack is drowned. Rose goes on to remarry. She never forgets her first love. At her death she glides up a glamorous staircase to eternity, where Jack, her truelove is waiting for her! That's quite a different version of events from the Bible, that I, for one, had subscribed to. As far as I was concerned, my love for Martin would stretch beyond the bounds of time. I would spend Eternity with him; the fact that he only lived just shy of three decades was not that significant, except for the memories we missed out on making, the children we might have had - we still would have eternity together! Yes, I believe we will, but not in the way I was expecting. We will recognise each other, but we will be in a totally different dimension; part of The Bride together, united in perfect holy love with all other believers, but fully focussed on Jesus. Such mind-boggling, deep and difficult concepts, but important to get an understanding of.

I remembered Martin's comments in bed, about me remarrying if anything ever happened to him. Marry someone else? Unthinkable! But Martin had given me his blessing to do so. At the time, I was cross with him for even suggesting it. Maybe he'd had a premonition? My head was reeling with deep questions swirling round like clothes in a washing machine. Biblically I was free to marry again, Martin had given his blessing, but I didn't want to, and I couldn't see it happening. Sometimes I would have vivid dreams that Martin had been away but had come back to me. I had mixed feelings about them. Being reunited with him was wonderful, but I was also cross with him for abandoning me and putting me through such a gruelling time. Why did he have to leave again? The crashing waves of reality would wake me with the dawn and leave me puzzled and disappointed. My emotions were in turmoil.

One morning I woke up to discover that my final hope of finding I was carrying Martin's child had been snuffed out. Another sadness! We should have got on with the fertility treatment, but we hadn't realised we had so little time. We had other things going on: over the span of our short marriage, we'd given a temporary home to various people who'd found themselves in need of a bolt hole. Some of these people had challenging circumstances, which required me to press more deeply into God's grace and count my blessings.

"God, why promise me a child if you're not going to fulfil it?"

Now there seemed little point carrying on with life. I missed Martin so much, and now there was no hope of having his child, I felt as though I had nothing to live for. I was not suicidal, I wasn't going to take my own life, but I was tired of living in a colourless existence with no prospects of happiness. I lay down on the bathroom floor where I'd found Martin that fateful night:

"Please God, you did it for him, now do it again for me. Beam me up please".

Nothing!

Several minutes elapsed.

"O.K! If you're not going to take me, please help me because I just can't see the point of living anymore. I want to be where Martin is!"

Time stood still. Something happened! A dream? A trance? Maybe in my imagination? I don't know, but I saw in my mind thick, dark clouds being parted and penetrated by a blinding shaft of pure white light which shone straight at me like a laser beam of love and healing. There was no sound, no voice but I was glued to the spot. I have no idea how long the experience lasted, but I knew something had happened deep in my soul and heart. Peace and joy bubbled up like a wellspring of pure, clear water. My broken heart was healed! I knew my life was not meant to end yet. I had a fresh sense of purpose. Slowly, I sat up and considered what had just happened. Amazing! Humbling, that God had heard me, actually heard me ... and had answered me in such a dramatic way. And, ...hang on! Yes, it was actually **thirty days** since Martin had died! It was not only my broken heart that had been healed, but this had galvanised my relationship with God, and for the first time, I felt pregnant, not with a child, but with the expectation of good things ahead. The negative, fear-whispering gremlin had been knocked off my shoulder and I was filled with hope. Now it all made sense, all those scriptures I had been led to read in my Bible had been there to prepare me for what was ahead. It was not lost on me either that Doreen's insistence that I teach at her school was the engineering of a higher power. Well done Doreen! Without her perseverance I would have been jobless now, and without an income: incredibly, I was too young to receive a widow's pension.

The following day a colleague from school, Ann, called with a bunch of flowers. They were daffodils and tulips.

" I know it's November, but these are just to let you know that Spring is coming!"

I appreciated their vibrant colours and the delicate freshness of their fragrance, and the words she spoke sparkled with hope and promise.

November! Hadn't I heard that something significant was suppose to happen then?

Later that evening, Pat, my prayer partner friend telephoned to see how I was. I told her about the flowers I'd received that afternoon and the reference to Spring. There was silence.

"Is everything alright?' I asked.

" Oh, er, well yes. Oh, now I'm going to have to tell you. I didn't want to upset you or overstep the mark.."

" What is it?" I asked impatiently.

"I was praying for you this morning, and I sensed the Lord gave me a verse for you from Song of Solomon. It's about the Winter being over and Spring coming"

" Wow, that's amazing" I bubbled out with a chuckle. "Let me tell you what happened in the bathroom yesterday…"

After our 'phone call, I found my Bible and read the verses she had given me. Excitement was welling up inside of me. What was God about to do next?

"Rise up, my love, my beautiful one, and come away. For behold, the winter is past. The rain is

over and gone. The flowers appear on the earth. The time of singing has come, and the voice of the turtle dove is heard in our land. The fig tree ripens her green figs. The vines are in blossom. They give out their fragrance. Arise my love, my beautiful one, and come away." (Song of Solomon 2:10-13)

Such rich, evocative words, brimming with the promise of fruitfulness and expectancy. My heart was buzzing! As I lay in bed that night, playing the events of the day over in my mind, I was truly thankful to God for His goodness. He'd met with me and healed me, and He'd sent two signs of confirmation that He was at work on my behalf and we were in a change of season together.

I walked up to the graveyard the next morning to visit Martin's grave. Although it was November, in my head the whole graveyard looked like a scene from Wordsworth's poem: 'I Wandered Lonely as a Cloud'; I could see in my mind, a blanket of glorious golden daffodils nodding their heads with joy in the breeze. Very strange! I had a strong sense of release. Words came into my head:

"You don't need to come here anymore. Martin isn't here. It's only his shell. He's alive with me."

And I remembered some words the angels spoke to the women who'd come to look for Jesus after his crucifixion. "Why do you look for the living among the dead? He is not here, but is risen (Luke 24:5-6). There was a sense of closure, but in a joyful, happy way.

The grave held the remains of Martin's body.

His spirit was safely resting with God.

My heart was healed, and I was on the cusp of something new. It may be November, but the cold grip of Winter's grief was thawing with the promise of Spring. Maybe, in a few years' time, a new relationship might come into bud. Maybe that's when my child of promise might be granted.

Chapter Nine

The Man From The Train

I was careful who I told about my experiences in the bathroom and churchyard. I realised some people were just not ready to hear it, and would be hurt and offended - it was certainly radical, and had taken me (Mrs Conventional) by surprise. One day Martin's mum Claire asked me if the beautiful roses she'd found by his grave were from me. I had to admit they were not, but commented, genuinely, that whoever had performed such a lovely gesture was very kind. I knew in my heart, that this new-found release from the expectations of others, and my accelerated healing, in no way undermined the deep love I had for Martin. I had done my best to love him in life, I had learned that disagreements had always to be sorted out quickly - certainly before bedtime; he was not a person you could be mad with for long. We had been a team.

A couple of weeks earlier, friends had taken me to choose a puppy from a litter of West Highland terriers from a farm in Lancashire. I was still feeling very low, but a certain little fellow climbed up onto my training shoe and started chewing my laces. I rather think that he had chosen me! So Toby was my new little companion, and around this time we went to collect him. It was rather a shock to the system for my cat, Tigger, who did not appreciate having her nose pushed out. I was glad that I was in a better frame of mind to enjoy Toby and my sense of joy was returning, so I was able to appreciate his antics. I had not expected to be the owner of a dog, and there were a few other things that I was not expecting to happen…

Not long after acquiring Toby, I came down with the flu and I was totally wiped out! My parents came over to look after us both because I did not have the energy to even go downstairs to let Toby out to do the necessaries. After a couple of days there was a visitor: a gentleman I'd never even spoken to, but who passed my house everyday as part of his routine. He was probably in his forties, smartly dressed and bearded. Incredibly my mum invited him in and sent him upstairs to my bedroom! I was in no fit state to receive visitors, either emotionally or physically: my nose was pulsating like I'd fought a boxing match and come off worst, I was sweaty and achy and not very good company at all. This was all very awkward. I subtly pulled the duvet as far up under my chin as I could manage, smiled weakly and tried to make small talk as he sat himself down on the end of the bed. After what seemed like an eon, he said his farewells and left. Relief! I didn't have any more visits from him, which I was pleased about. I'm sure he was a really lovely person, but I wasn't wanting to invite his attention.

There was another unsuitable suitor on the scene: once I had recovered and was back at work, I came home one day to discover a bunch of flowers on my front step with a message from a man who had recently started attending my church. The note informed me that he would pick me up at 7.30 to take me for a meal. There were no contact details, so I felt backed into a corner. There was no way that I was going to fulfil his wishes. My only option was to 'phone one of my church leaders and ask him to get in touch with this man and tell him not to call. Thankfully, he didn't turn up! I was hoping this wasn't going to become a regular occurrence; fending off unwanted attentions...but all of a sudden, thoughts started creeping into my head - well images rather than thoughts. I began thinking about the man on the train! It was very disconcerting - I didn't want to be thinking about him, and I asked God to help me stop.

"This is awful, God! I don't want to be doing this. For heaven's sake!"

But I could not shake them off, and to make matters worse, I would feel a teenage surge of excitement every time he came to mind. This started happening regularly.

One evening, about 6.30, not long after the 'bathroom experience' the doorbell rang. Who could this be? I laid aside the very complicated cross-stitch picture I was working on (bought specifically to keep me occupied through the long, dark evenings), and went to answer the door. I could not have been more shocked!! There, on the doorstep, carrying a bunch of red spray carnations was John - the man from the train!

"Hello, erm, I'm John. I'm here on behalf of my church." He held out the flowers.

I received them with delight and, rather shyly, I invited him in.

My heart was pounding in my chest. This was surreal. I felt as though I was in a dream. We made our way into the kitchen to make a cup of tea, Toby, my puppy, decided to introduce himself; then we went back to the lounge. Conversation flowed freely and as I looked at him, it was as if the word 'INTEGRITY' was written over his head. This was a man who was trustworthy and honourable. I felt completely safe with him. I was confident that he had no ulterior motives.

He told me he had been sent by his church, as he lived the nearest to me. He'd really been so affected by my situation, he'd prayed harder than he'd ever prayed before. He offered to help me with any practicalities. It turned out that he was a single man and lived with his ageing parents, supporting his mum as she cared for his father who had Parkinson's disease. After a couple of hours, he took his leave. I reflected on how different he looked: relaxed in his jeans, blue checked shirt and blue lamb's wool sweater, instead of his smart, official-looking Banker's suit.

Well! What a really lovely man! The voice of reason spoke up: "Yes, but he came round as a representative of his church, right! He has no romantic aspirations whatsoever!" That was true, but as I got into bed, I sensed God directing me to read the Book of Ruth, so over the next few nights, that's what I did.

The story of Ruth starts with a Jewish couple, Elimelech and his wife Naomi, moving to Moab with their two sons because of famine in their home town of Bethlehem. Their sons married Moabite girls: Ruth and Orpah. Sadly, Elimelech died, followed by his two sons, leaving the three women alone and childless. Naomi, bereft and barren, decided to return home because she'd heard that the situation in Bethlehem had improved. She offered her daughters-in-law their freedom to go and find new husbands, but Ruth refused to leave her, and accompanied her back to Bethlehem:

"Ruth said, "Don't urge me to leave you, and to return from following you, for where you go, I will go; and where you stay, I will stay. Your people will be my people, and your God my God. Where you die, I will die, and there I will be buried. May the LORD do so to me, and more also, if anything but death parts you and me". (Ruth 1: 16-17)

So, having returned, Ruth went to glean (pick barley) in the fields of Naomi's late husband's wealthy relative, Boaz. This was a Jewish custom, that farmers would leave the edges of their fields unharvested, so that the poor could pick the barley for themselves.

Boaz noticed the new young woman in his fields and made enquiries about her. Finding out she was a relative, he sent her a message to exclusively glean in his fields only, and gave his workers instructions to look after her and show her favour by leaving extra sheaves of barley for her to gather.

When Naomi heard how gracious and generous Boaz had been to Ruth, she was hopeful that he would do the honourable thing, according to their culture, and 'redeem' Ruth, by marrying her. (I'm guessing this was all new to Ruth, because she was a Gentile and not familiar with Jewish protocol). She instructed Ruth to put her glad rags on and go to the threshing floor at night, where Boaz would be. She was to climb under his blanket, and lie at his feet - this would indicate to him that she was inviting him to find her a husband, or marry her himself. (Wow! What vulnerability!).

This must have touched Boaz's heart, as he sent her home with a bundle of barley and the promise that he would sort things out. There was another relative - an old man - who had first refusal; happily he did not want the responsibility of a young wife, so he relinquished his claim. Boaz married Ruth, and not long after, Naomi was blessed with a grandson: Ruth, a woman and a 'foreigner', ends up in the lineage of Jesus! (See Matthew 1:5).

Wow! What an amazingly powerful story. I could see the parallels in my own situation: widowed at an early age and childless. I recalled some words that Naomi had said to Ruth after she'd returned from her midnight encounter: "Just be patient, and wait and see how all this turns out" (Ruth 3:18).

I wrote a letter to the people at John's church, thanking them for their prayers and the flowers. I asked a friend to post it through John's letterbox. I wondered if it would generate a further response. I was feeling betwixt and between. Martin, I knew was resting in peace, I was still in "the expected time of mourning", but God had miraculously healed me, I could not deny it. Could he now really be saying it was time for those tiny, new, green shoots of hope to start springing up for me?

John kept in contact with me, and was very sensitive to my position; in fact he had no romantic agenda whatsoever, and was genuinely there to help me with practical issues. In fact that in itself was very disarming and attractive. He was quite courageous to help me: I'm sure there must have been whisperings and assumptions about his attentions towards a newly widowed woman - but it did not deter him from showing me kindness.

One of the topics of our conversations had been about transparency in relationships; how it's important to be honest and truthful. The need for this was becoming more and more apparent as I was beginning to fall in love with him, and it was something I could not stop.

One morning, the radio alarm burst into life with a punchy Latino tune by Gloria Estefan And The Miami Sound Machine: 'Get On Your Feet'. It was an encouragement to be proactive. Hmm! I remembered the story of Ruth climbing under Boaz's blanket, and gasped at the outrageousness of this thought, but I decided I would go low key and make John a special Christmas card, thanking him for his companionship, and post it through his letterbox myself! Honestly, I felt like a schoolgirl with a crush on her teacher, but yes, I would do it in the afternoon before he got home from work, so I didn't have to see him. I recalled Naomi's advice to Ruth to be patient and see how all this works out.

Christmas card clutched in my hand, I got in my car and drove to John's house, parking on the road, not the drive. I walked up the path, past the neatly manicured lawn towards the 1950's semi-detached house. Furtively crouching down to post my offering through the letterbox at the base of the porch door, I was spotted through the frosted glass! The door was opened by a friendly, dignified lady in her late seventies. Her hair was in the style of Queen Elizabeth II and she wore a fine checkered house-coat to protect her neat blouse and skirt.

"Hello Love", she trilled.

"Oh, hello. I er was just posting this card for John'" I limply replied, feeling rather foolish.

"Come in Love"

I didn't feel like I could refuse. I was ushered into a neat and cosy room. A roaring fire in the grate gave a rosy glow to the face of the old man sitting in an armchair beside it: John's father. I was offered a seat in the armchair on the other side of the fireplace, and soon had a China cup and saucer filled with steaming tea placed in my hands.

"John will be home soon", announced his mother (Hilda), and disappeared into the kitchen to complete her culinary tasks. I made small talk with John's father (Allan): a man of tall stature, a gentleman, I could tell. He was struggling with the tremors of Parkinson's disease, but was doing his best to engage me in conversation - I liked him instantly.

I heard the front door click open. Oh heck! I felt a bit embarrassed. My plan had gone awry. All this fuss over a Christmas card. John entered the room, he looked mildly surprised to see me. We exchanged a polite greeting. I feebly explained why I was in his parents' house, and then, as his evening meal was being placed on the table, I made my way out thanking his mum for the tea.

I scurried down the path silently scolding myself: " It hadn't turned out like Ruth and Boaz. Silly girl to think it would! No armfuls of barley or honourable pledges! Baaah! Shake it off and try and retain some dignity". But I felt as if I'd jumped into a deep puddle with both feet and well and truly muddied the waters! I hoped I hadn't spoiled our friendship!

Chapter Ten

Transparency: The Chips Are Down!

My parents were over for a visit, and it just so happened that John had invited me to accompany him to a country pub for a Christmas meal with some of his church friends. I was relieved that he still wanted to be involved with me, but I was a bit tentative about how things stood between us. Would it be overthinking things to wonder if, by introducing me to his friends, there was a possibility that our relationship was becoming more than platonic? I had the conversations regarding 'Transparency' permanently hovering in my mind. I was impatient to know what was happening, but also a little nervous.

It was lovely to have the opportunity to get dressed up for an evening out, but I had spent ages deliberating what to wear. I opted for smart casual. Despite my healing, I was newly widowed and I was conscious of the possible mutual awkwardness this evening could present. There were many questions whirring in my head like a washing machine on spin cycle. However, I was pleased that my parents would have the opportunity of meeting John. I knew it would put their minds at rest to see that he was a very decent and trustworthy person and had no wicked agenda to seduce me.

The doorbell sounded. Deep breath, this was it! My Dad answered the door, and gregariously offered his hand in greeting, announcing himself with enthusiasm:

" Dennis, Dennis Harrison, You must be John!"

I couldn't help smiling, proud at my dad's usual warmth and friendliness, although I felt a bit like a teenager going on a date leaving my parents at home twiddling their fingers until my safe arrival at the end of the evening.

John commented in the car that he had been mischievously temped to respond to my Dad's greeting with "Taxi for Hughes?" (my then surname).

So we arrived and I was introduced to people. They all knew who I was and what I had been through, although no-one mentioned it. I was wondering what people were really thinking, what assumptions they were making; it was all a bit overwhelming. They were quite a riotous bunch of Scousers, extremely exuberant and with a unique sense of humour, more so than what I was used to. My own church friends were fun-loving and cheerful, but in a more demure way. I coped by withdrawing into my shell and just observing.

The food arrived, and John was particularly enjoying the crispy French fries on his plate. He commented that his mother made fantastic chips, and strongly implied that he could never leave home unless his future wife could make chips like his mother. Just a throw away line, seemingly insignificant, but to oversensitive me, it was loaded with meaning and hit me like a bullet: "He's happy as he is, he has no romantic interest in me, what am I even doing here? I don't want to be here out of sympathy!" I fought back scalding tears and made my excuses to find the Ladies room. I had to compose myself, and fast. Unfortunately, I was dependent on a lift home and I did not want to draw attention to myself or cause any embarrassment to spoil the evening for others. I endured the rest of the evening but I was desperate to get home to my bolthole. Like the solitary mason bee, I was more comfortable solving issues in private isolation; I would have to dodge my parents' questions when I got home, but in bed I would be able to silently sob away my disappointment and frustration at my own foolish imaginings.

My Mum was not one for engaging in deep conversations, but the following morning, having seen how crestfallen I was, she asked me what was wrong. I told her I'd misread the signs about John and I was feeling stupid and confused. She asked me if I loved him. I had no hesitation in saying that I did. Honestly, it was remarkable to have that conversation with my mum. It was like a catalyst: I knew what I had to do! I had to be transparent! The next opportunity I got, I would metaphorically declare my hand. Once John knew the depth of my feelings he would be free to decide what to do next: pursue or back away. I had to give him that option, it was crunch time, and it was risky. I would be seeing John again at the weekend. We were going to a Christmas concert: Graham Kendrick's Make Way For Christmas (The Gift). I asked John to come and collect me half an hour early as I had something to tell him…

My parents had already returned home to Hull, so I was alone in the house again. I was pacing the floor waiting for the knock on the door. Eventually, the moment arrived and I invited John in. I think he thought it was all very 'cloak and dagger'. I sat him down on the sofa and started my well rehearsed speech:

" You know how we've talked about being transparent?", I ventured. "Well, I've got to be transparent with you now,... I'm falling in love with you." I was all geared up to tell him he could say goodbye now and we'd call it a day...

"What did you say?" He looked pretty stunned. Flipping heck! Did I really have to say it again?

"I'm falling in love with you."

After a moment of letting those words sink in, he looked at me and said, "Can I kiss you?"

Bells and streamers! Of course I said yes. I knew he wouldn't have asked if he wasn't reciprocating my feelings. Love had been awakened in him! We looked at each other sheepishly and giggled. "What are we going to do now?" I asked. We decided to keep things under wraps until we had been able to tell parents and in-laws. I didn't want them to find out through hearsay. It was difficult though, because new love is like a bubbling stream, it's just so hard trying to conceal its rapturous joy.

We went to the concert, and in the car I told him how his comments regarding chips had knocked me for six. Fortunately for him, I'm quite good at making chips, and all sorts of other culinary delights his dear mum wouldn't even attempt, curries for example, and other such delicious cuisines that she would have called "mollucks deloo".

That night, as I lay in bed, I was so giddy I could barely contain myself. What a wonderful thing God had done! I remembered the story of Ruth, and I had to say sorry to God that I had so easily taken my eyes off the ball and not trusted His words and promises. I was thankful to Him, that even though I had been focussed on circumstances and how things appeared, He did not withhold this amazing blessing from us. How precious is His loving kindness.

The following day was Sunday, so we both attended our respective churches. We met again in the evening. John came round to my house. Snuggled together uncomfortably on the two seater sofa, John asked me a question: "If I was to ask you to marry me, what would you say?" I replied that I would say yes, so he'd better not ask me yet. Honestly, we could have got married there and then, but I was conscious of how utterly shocking this would be for people. I was shocked! God had certainly accelerated things. And without a shadow of a doubt, it was God that had done this, but other people might not see it that way. We had to tread carefully and sensitively.

The transparent conversation continued that evening. It now was appropriate to tell John about my prognosis from the STD clinic*, and he told me things that he was not proud of and had shared remorsefully with his trusted friend. It didn't matter to either of us. We both knew the Grace of God's forgiveness in our lives, and we extended it to each other. We had no secrets from each other, but we did have our own sweet secret, and at the right moment we would reveal it.

* Amazingly, although I'd just been through bereavement- probably the most stressful experience ever, I had not had a single outbreak of herpes since being prayed for. Praise God.

Chapter Eleven

The Golden Thread

It was the week before Christmas and I was due to go over to my parents in Hull. I was keen to bring key people up to date with our news.

My parents were relieved that I had found new love and that they had already had the opportunity to meet John.

Martin's parents were equally delighted for us. Amazingly, one of Claire's closest friends had been John's primary schoolteacher, and had commented on what a lovely, polite little boy he had been (over thirty years ago!). That had been enough to satisfy Claire of his suitability.

John's parents were glad he'd potentially found his wife. I think it must have been a bittersweet reaction for his mum. She had endured such trouble to have him, her life revolved around him. She would miss looking after him. She had been widowed and childless before she met Allan; and she had suffered several miscarriages before she fell pregnant with John at the age of forty.

We'd been through the same sadnesses, which I'm sure helped engender her approval of me.

John too, had his own backstory:

After a broken engagement several years earlier, John had been on a quest to find his life partner. He joined a Christian postal dating site (this was way before online dating was available), and had arranged to meet a young lady near Preston. While she was visiting the Ladies' room, he sensed a voice in his head asking him: "What are you doing here? You won't find your wife this way!" He cancelled his subscription to that organisation, but still the search continued. The years rolled by with several relationships. After ending yet another, the pastor's wife had an encouragement for John after the Sunday morning service. She told him that his partner would cross his tracks (John and I had our first encounters on the train into Liverpool Central). Who said God doesn't have a sense of humour!

Several months later, John decided to call on a lovely Christian lady whom he knew from previous church events. She had been divorced a couple of years earlier. Maybe now she would be ready to pursue another relationship? Alas, his plans were thwarted; she wasn't in when he called. He went back to his car, frustrated, angry and grumbling at God. He must have been so weary and disappointed, but every complaint he uttered received the same response: "Trust Me". It was an audible voice; calm and patient.

How remarkable, that several months later, when calling round to deliver flowers from his church, there was no romantic agenda, and yet this was the fulfilment of his destiny. I have discovered, along with John, that it's only when we give things over to God, and stop trying to fix them ourselves that He sorts things out so much better than we could ever have hoped for. There, behind the scenes, over years and months God was weaving things together with His golden thread. He is always at work, His timing is perfect and nothing ever takes Him by surprise.

Christmas Eve 1989 was a Sunday. I accompanied my parents to church on the Sunday morning. I was so grateful to God that my Christmas had been transformed from what I had been expecting a few weeks earlier. As I was visiting the Ladies' room, I overheard two elderly ladies discussing me. They'd known me from childhood, as I attended Sunday School there.

"I see Rosemary's here today. What a shame. She'll never get over it, you know!"

I thought to myself, "Jesus, you have got me through this. I am over it, over the sadness and grief. I'm sorry that this is not everyone's experience, that so many people are stuck in the mire of grief for the rest of their days. But you have turned my sorrow into joy"

When I returned home, and the news was out, there were many people who shared our joy. People who knew us well were absolutely certain that this was God's doing and they marvelled at it. Others were not so generous. There were single ladies who complained to my face it was unfair that I "should get two bites at the cherry". Others were prickly or cool, and definitely avoided me. Having been a people-pleaser most of my life, I decided I was not going to allow their thoughts or opinions to spoil the wonderful joy that God had brought us. Would people actually prefer me to wear black for the rest of my days? Yes, I realised that they were still in mourning for Martin, but God had engineered this new season, He had prepared me for it and shown me His heart in the Bible passages He'd led me to. If they didn't like it, they should take their complaints to Him.

Something disturbing did start to happen once John and I had got together: I started having dreams about Martin. After Martin's passing, I welcomed such dreams as it made me feel close to him and comforted, but now they caused me disquiet. The essence was that he had gone away, had abandoned me, and now he had come back when I had started a new relationship; it put me in a dilemma. There was no one I felt able to talk to about this. What was I to do? I knew deep down that God had healed me, I wholeheartedly welcomed my new and wonderful beginning with John, so why was this happening? I felt guilty that I was annoyed with Martin for coming back to spoil things, and also for abandoning me in the first place (although I knew he hadn't really had the choice about what had happened).

When in doubt, turn to the Bible. It had been my guide so far and helped me navigate the unchartered waters of bereavement. I came across a verse in Ecclesiastes which urges people to remember their Creator before they get old and their bodies become infirm, before "the silver cord (of life) is severed" (Ecclesiastes 12:6) for:

".. the dust returns to the earth as it was, and the spirit returns to God who gave it." (Ecc12 v7)

At death a person's spirit returns to God. They are not free to wander the earth or come back into the lives of their loved ones. They have gone into a different realm. Just as a newly born child, when birthed from the womb into the world, has its umbilical cord severed, so it is with death. The baby cannot return to the womb; the departed cannot return to the world. The good news for those who believe in the death and resurrection of Jesus, is that He conquered death, which came into the world through sin, enabling us to experience eternal life in the glory of heaven as ransomed, forgiven souls (see John 3:16). I know many people have sensed the presence of their departed loved ones, and this has brought them comfort. I can relate to that myself; however, it can create a sense of deep longing to reconnect more fully, but trying to love a spirit in the same way you loved the physical person is just too frustrating, if at all possible. I would warn against trying to reconnect with loved ones through well meaning psychics and mediums. It may be very convincing that they have reconnected, but it could be a cruel deception by the forces of darkness. Only Jesus has the keys to death: he regained them from Satan when he conquered death at the Resurrection. Satan no longer has the authority, but he acts as though he has. The Bible warns us not to engage in such practices, no matter how desperate we feel, because it could potentially open up a doorway to a whole load of trouble for us (Leviticus 19:31, 1 John4:1 for starters).

Another trait of our adversary, Satan, the enemy of God, is that he wants to disturb our peace and spoil every good thing that God has planned for us. He is a deceiver, in fact Jesus called him "the father of lies" (John 8:44) and his plan is to bring confusion, guilt and disruption into our lives. He acts illegally, but God has given us authority over him through the name of Jesus (see Matt 28:18, John16:24, Phil 2:(-11). Revisiting this revelation brought me peace and clarity. Martin had given me his blessing to marry again. He was now in a different realm and when I next meet him, he will be as a dear, beloved brother. There was one more thing that I needed to do in order to be fully free to pursue my relationship with John, and once again, God the great engineer, made a path for me to find it.

My parents were over for a visit, and we heard that there was a praise and worship meeting being held in a church in Crosby which we decided to attend. It was actually quite unusual for my parents to do this, but anyhow, we went along. During the course of the evening, one of the leaders of the church announced that they sensed there where people who needed to have *soul-ties broken. I immediately felt that was for me, although I wasn't entirely sure what it meant. I made my way down to the front of the building where two lovely ladies prayed with me. I felt a release, and I didn't have anymore unwanted dreams after that. The theory became my reality.

*When two people are joined together in like heart and mind, and also intimately, they form a soul-tie. They are knitted together, which in marriage is a good thing. That covenant is only valid until the death of one of the partners; however, there may still be an emotional attachment. Subconsciously, remnants of me were clinging onto Martin, even though the covenant we had was ended. A bit like clinging onto the string of a helium balloon, I had to fully let it go, break off, be released from any remaining emotional ties, so that I was fully free to pursue my new relationship with John in a healthy way, and bring closure for Martin to be fully released into his new realm. I also wanted to deal with that sense of abandonment, and so I refuted the lie that Martin had left me. He had been a loving and faithful husband. Sometimes we are unaware of how deeply rooted the bonds we make are, which can affect our future relationships if we don't deal with them safely. To use a theatrical metaphor, I didn't want John to be waiting in the wings like an understudy, but for him to come onto the main stage and fully play his part. This was Act 2; the curtain needed to come down on Act 1, although it had been wonderful: Jesus makes all things new.

Jesus said, *"You will know the truth, and the truth will make you free."*

(John 8:32)

Chapter Twelve

A New Chapter Begins

Deeply in love, we were so enjoying getting to know each other and making plans for our future together. We had decided that we would get engaged in the early Spring and married in the Autumn: that would give people a full year to get used to us being a couple. Although no dates were yet circled on the calendar, the fact it would happen was a certainty.

One day in late January, I had arranged to go out for lunch with a friend called Nina (not her real name). We went to a lovely hotel near Ormskirk, called Briars Hall. After our meal, Nina went to the Ladies room and I sat taking in the surroundings: "This would be a great venue for a wedding reception", I thought to myself. The appeal of the place grew in my mind, so I decided to make enquiries. I went to the reception desk and asked about the availability for a wedding reception. It would need to tie in with school holiday dates, so the weekend before Autumn half term would be the only possible option.

"When were you thinking for?' Asked the receptionist.

"November?"

"Which November?"

She started flicking through the pages of the desk diary.

"This November."

She looked at me over the top of her spectacles, with a doubtful expression.

"Oh, there won't be any chance of this November. We're fully booked up for this year and even into next year. Wait, I'll just check. What date would it be?

I quickly worked out the date of the weekend before the half term holidays.

"It would need to be the 10th." I said with hope waning.

She found the page: "Well, I don't believe it! It seems we've had a cancellation for that day."

"Will you pencil me in then, please?" My heart was popping. I went back to our table and tried to look as nonchalant as possible, as if nothing had happened, but inside I was full of glee and thanking God for this mini miracle. Did this seem rather forward of me? Maybe a tad controlling and manipulative? I was not given to such bold moves. I saw it as an act of faith; God graciously confirming that our plans to marry in the Autumn were on track.

Waiting for John to call round that evening was joyously unbearable. Again, I'll reiterate, this was before mobile phones. We had no instant means of communication, but anyway, I wanted to tell him face to face. When he came through the front door, I had a smile from ear to ear, and I must have looked pretty smug.

"Guess what I did today?" I asked, knowing he would never guess.

"I've no idea, but you're going to tell me".

"I provisionally booked our wedding reception!", I announced, trilling off into delighted laughter as I watched the astonishment on his face. I related the amazing story, and told him that I would wait for the official marriage proposal, but at least we'd made a start with the plans!

The same thing happened with my wedding outfit. I took a trip with Pat, the lady who gave me the Scripture that winter was past. We went shopping in Manchester during half term, and I came back with my wedding dress! It was quite a demure 1920's style outfit, and fitted me perfectly, so it wouldn't require any alterations and as it was not bulky, I was able to bring it home in a carrier bag. It had been a crazy day, and we were full of giggles. We got the wrong train home and were heading to Blackpool instead of Liverpool, but all we could do was roll around laughing 'til our sides ached. People must have thought we'd been drinking.

Eventually, John did do the "down on one knee" proposal, and we laughed because so much was already in place. The reaction to our news was divided across two poles. Some people were delighted and excited for us, others were not. That made us sad, but we were confident that God had ordained our union. The decade I had enjoyed with Martin had been wonderful, but that chapter now had closed and God was graciously allowing us to find happiness and purpose together. I know it's very unusual for grieving to be so short, and in saying all this, I don't want to minimise how awful or lengthy the experience can be for many people, but all I can say is this is how God clearly moved in our situation. We chose to flow with His timing.

I was actually bowled over by the goodness of God, and found that a new confidence was growing in my relationship with Him. I was seeing how He was involved with every detail of our lives and it was building my faith and trust in Him. I was no longer expecting things to go wrong, but enjoying the blessings He was sending. I also was mindful of the small, usually taken-for-granted things. I particularly enjoyed seeing the snowdrops that year. How amazing they are; first to push up through the hard, frozen earth and yet they are pristine in their dazzling white fragility. They have become a symbol of perseverance for me: God's strength enabling us to overcome weakness. Easter too, was particularly poignant and meaningful. I danced in church on Easter Sunday because of the marvellous and wonderful truth that Jesus had died and risen again from the dead. He had conquered death forever and, if we believe, we will all one day be reunited with our loved ones for evermore.

We were sharing our time between John's church and mine, but, inevitably the choice would have to be made: which one would we attend once we were married? Some people, out of an understandable emotional response, put us under a bit of pressure and left us in a quandary. They were telling us where they believed God wanted us to attend. Fortunately, John's longstanding, wise friend Rob, who with his wife, Ann had been a great support to him during his singleness, had good advice. Without any attempt to persuade or coerce, Rob simply said that the Holy Spirit does not bring confusion. That was all we needed to hear. I was reminded of Ruth's exhortation to her mother in law, Naomi, that she would follow her wherever she went. That's what I would do with John. Also, I believed it would be wiser for me go to his church as his new wife, rather than he come to my church as my new husband, where there would inevitably be comparisons between him and Martin. I was adamant that I didn't want that, but it's a human trait; people tend to look back at how things used to be, we often resist change. Also, I believe that God often uses others to confirm the thoughts He has already sown into our hearts and minds first; that confirmation, alongside

Biblical principles, resonates with our spirit that it's the right course to take.

So, regrettably, we had to amicably step away from people who, although trying to be kind, were actually trying to push us into <u>their</u> desired outcome. It was difficult to resist, but we were determined not to let this happen - this was a new chapter for us both, the old had gone and we needed space to discover each other and embrace this fresh beginning. As much as I loved my church family, I didn't want John living in Martin's shadow - <u>he</u> wasn't about to let that happen either. We hoped that our union might facilitate the coming together of both congregations in joint events and social activities.

There were also some tensions involving family too. There were three mothers to placate: my own, John's and my former mother-in-law, each with their own great characteristics, each needing to be considered, and to say it was challenging is an understatement. In fact it became a bit of a blight that one night it almost finished us:

We had just eaten our evening meal at John's parents' house. The conversation focussed on arrangements for the wedding. Trying to please everyone had my head reeling. I abruptly got up from the table and left for home. Before I'd driven very far, I knew I'd been rash, but I stubbornly continued my journey home, wondering how John would react to this first blip. I got out the ironing board and vented my spleen on the pile of laundry that was waiting to be ironed. I knew I would need to make contact again once I'd calmed down. Then, I heard a car pull up outside the house, a quick check at the window confirmed it was John. I was so relieved. He had pursued me: it was what I needed; we made amends.

Talking things through we came to the conclusion that we couldn't please everyone, even family members. Change and adjustment are often mutually painful, we need to hold people lightly and be able to forgive when we get hurt, compromised or misunderstood. I was certainly sorry for any unintentional hurt I might have caused by my actions, but sometimes we need to take a step back and breathe deeply. For once I was actually glad that God, in His wisdom, had not enabled me to have Martin's babies. Decisions would have been even more complicated and delicate if I'd had to consider the feelings of my children, although I realise many families face such sensitive challenges. I'm glad He loves us enough to know what is good for us as individuals and doesn't give in to our tantrums.

The decision that we would be attending John's church meant that we would need to look for a new home in Maghull. We started our search in April. Maghull is a suburb of Liverpool and stands on the Leeds to Liverpool canal. It was once a small village centred around agricultural land, but has steadily expanded. There are a few streets of houses built after the First World War, but most of it is post Second World War and modern housing estates. John saw a notice in the local paper for a 1930s house for private sale backing onto the canal. The vendors were an elderly couple, Dorothy and Arthur, and they raised the bar when it came to selling houses! We were greeted with warm, freshly baked scones and florentines and steaming tea served in china cups. It was like visiting a favourite aunty. Arthur had evidently been a dab hand at DIY, and the place was beautifully maintained, if a little dated for our taste. We made an offer, which was accepted, even though my house was not yet on the market.

I was a little uncomfortable about putting my house on the market with an estate agent: having to show people round on my own. I didn't need to worry. God already had the situation covered.

Martin had been very fond of classic cars. He had bought one - a Triumph Stag which kept losing its hubcaps! A beautiful car, but not really my style. I sold it and bought a Fiat Uno! There was still a Mercedes Gullwing to sell. One evening, one of John's old acquaintances invited us for a meal. He and his wife were intrigued by the news that John was finally tying the knot. Dave, our host, was quite keen on cars and the Mercedes came up in conversation. Dave said he may be interested, but he had a friend who would definitely be interested, so we exchanged contact details and arranged a viewing. A couple of weeks later, Dave and his friend Albie called round to view the car. He loved it but didn't feel he could stretch to it because he was looking to buy a new house. I told him I was selling my house, and he was very interested; contacting his solicitor on the Monday morning. Amazing! I was so glad that I hadn't got to go through all the stress of finding a buyer. It would be sad to leave that home, especially as Martin had improved it so much with a lovely new kitchen extension and loft conversion, But our new home would be lovely too, and where our adventure would begin as a married couple.

It was now August 1990. The Berlin Wall had just been dismantled, and I was due to go on a trip to Germany with my friend Pat and a man from John's church. The trip had been arranged by a church from Tubingen in former West Germany. The contrast between West and the former East Germany was stark and shocking. This was an amazing opportunity to introduce people to the love of God. Of course, living in a Communist country, people had been told all their lives that God is dead. I remembered a smattering of German from my secondary school days, but it was enough to get by. I recall an old lady in the market square still policed by Russian soldiers. She had tears in her eyes. She was a Christian, and said she had been praying for forty years to be able to talk about Jesus in public. Wow! That is persevering prayer! On another occasion we went to an estate of oppressive, grey high rise apartments. One of the German team, Ruben, started playing his guitar while the rest of us sang. After a couple of minutes, children started streaming out of the buildings and running towards our group, laughing and smiling with great excitement. It was like a scene from the pied piper of Hamelin. So beautiful. They had been drawn to our joyful singing like moths to a candle flame. There were many other moving and challenging moments on that trip: the kindness and generosity of people with so little, who are prepared to share all they have with strangers. However, I was very much anticipating getting home. I had missed John so much, and I was looking forward to signing all the paperwork for the sale of my house.

When I arrived home, John greeted me with a question:

"Do you want to know the good news or the bad news?"

As always, I like to get the bad news out of the way first. The bad news was that the sale of my house had fallen through because Albie's buyer had pulled out! I was crestfallen...

The good new was that Albie's solicitor, who was a friend of his, loved the house, wanted to buy it and had all the paperwork in place! Yahoo!

Lying in bed that night, once again I thanked God for His amazing goodness. And as I thought about everything I'd been through: bereavement, selling a house, new relationship, it occurred to me that'd I'd not had a single further attack of herpes since the first one way back. I'm sure it was the general rule that it should be in a person's cells for life, but it seemed that God had healed me, or was certainly holding it back. He's the 'God of the Impossible', He's the God who heals.

Chapter Thirteen

The Big Day Approaches

The contracts for our house moves were signed, and I took up lone residence in our new home before the beginning of the Autumn term. Our vendors were happy to be ensconced into their new accommodation near to their son. We had a couple of months to get it redecorated and buy some new furniture before the wedding: exciting times.

The weeks passed by, and we busily finalised all the plans and logistics for our wedding day: We were looking for some entertainment for our evening reception, and friends had recommended a jazz band called 'Serendipity'. They were playing at a hotel in Southport, so we went along with another couple to hear them. They were very good, so we booked them. Afterwards, as we were sauntering along Lord Street looking in shop windows, we came across a bridal shop. John pointed to a pair of shoes in the window; they were ivory satin, 1920's style with a curved, Louis heel, and buckle fastening.

" Oh what horrible shoes!", he exclaimed. "There like something my Granny would wear!"

Quite surprised that he should hold such strong feelings about them, I felt duty bound to inform him that I had purchased an identical pair as part of my wedding outfit. I loved them, and I wasn't going to change them. There was an awkward moment, then we laughed. He would just have to remember not to look at my feet!

After much deliberating, the sensitive job of finalising the guest list was completed. A few people declined, even without an RSVP, but that was their choice and one has to forgive, try to understand and move on. Most were happy and excited to accept. Finally, the service was organised, with friends from both our church families involved with the music and formalities. I had started attending John's church more regularly now, as our house was in that neighbourhood. I was looking forward to John moving in after the wedding. It had been so challenging living apart.

It's a tradition, of course for bride and groom to undergo the preliminaries of their wedding day with a 'hen' or 'stag do', respectively.

My 'hen do' was a meal at a local Chinese restaurant with ladies from both churches. I felt rather nervous, because I was afraid that the rather more daring Maghull contingency would organise a 'surprise' which might not go down too well with the more demure Ormskirk ladies. Sadly, I could hardly eat a thing, my tummy was turning like a cement mixer. I was hoping and praying there would not be anything excruciatingly embarrassing to endure, such as a kiss-o-gram (a popular feature of 90's parties - a hunk in fancy dress). My over- fertile imagination was put at ease. I just had a package to open which turned out to be lingerie - not so bad!

John did not get away so lightly. His 'stag do' involved just the men from his church, so there was no calming influence, although I had strongly urged Rob, his best man, to be gentle with him - he was approaching 40 years of age, which seemed significant! The tradition was to subject the groom to a dousing in the Leeds Liverpool canal, but this was November! It would have been at the very least extremely cold, if not frozen over. I made Rob promise that wouldn't happen. Instead, after a meal together, they all made their way back to our new home. (I had made myself scarce: a girl's movie night with chocolate cake). John was then dragged into the garden, stripped naked and covered with tomato ketchup, desiccated coconut, custard powder and other things out of my cupboards. Needless to say, Toby, my little dog was totally bemused by their wild antics. Fortunately, I left it long enough before returning home, and all evidence of their mischief had been removed. At least John had been spared the murky depths of the canal!

On the eve of our wedding, my parents, two sisters and their families came from Hull for supper at our house. John met them briefly. He called in before going for a much more civilised evening than his previous hijinks: curry with Rob. Kindly, friends had offered accommodation to my family. My parents stayed with me.

The morning of the wedding had a much different feel from my first wedding day. Then, there had been a houseful of people needing to get ready, including my sisters' 5 year old daughters who were bridesmaids along with Martin's sisters. I was the last to get ready, dragging a brush through my hair, frantically slapping on my makeup and needing my Dad to fumble, fastening the many tiny pearl buttons on the back of my dress. Of course , I was much younger the first time round, but sure of my love for Martin.

This time, aged 30, there was a totally different feel: a luxurious soak in the bath, ladies coming to do hair and makeup, for me and my bridesmaid, Kaggs. A much calmer experience altogether.

One of the issues I had to contend with after Martin's death, was to do with the VAT office. Martin had been self employed, and so required to pay this tax. I had duly informed them of Martin's passing, but was told that I would be required to pay according to the previous year's earnings (even though there was no income coming into the business), and then claim it back. I am pretty inept at money matters, and I found this situation very frustrating and uncompassionate, but I had to comply with it. How wonderful that John, with his financial know-how, was able to help me through all this.

One of the most significant people to arrive at my house that Saturday morning was the postman. He was bearing a brown envelope from the VAT office. Against my better judgement, I opened it and read its contents. It informed me that I had been de-registered from their books. I let out a cheer! How wonderful, that today of all days, I should receive that letter. It was a final break with the past: a new beginning! Thank you God!

Clothed in my beautiful outfit, including 'Granny's shoes', my Dad escorted me to the waiting wedding car to start our journey to the church. This was it. My Winter was over: although it was November, for me it was Springtime.

It was raining, and the chauffeur sheltered me with a large white umbrella as I walked into the building. My Dad was beaming, I think he was just so happy and relieved that he had another opportunity to hand me over to a good, loving man. The music started, I focussed on John, looking very handsome, waiting for me at the front. I arrived by his side. Our eyes met:

"You look stunning" he whispered with a smile.

"I've been de-registered!" I replied.

One of our wedding hymns was 'Tell Out My Soul', a beautiful hymn based on Mary's song of praise when she visited her relative, Elisabeth, who was also expecting a miracle baby later on in life. (see Luke1:46-55). I'd sung this a few months earlier at a Women's World Day of Prayer event, and the words just struck me so strongly: God is faithful and mighty, he does wonderful exploits in people's lives and He promises to reveal His love down the generations. This was now my experience, and it filled me with immense gratitude and wonder.

Chapter Fourteen

The Honeymoon Is Over

Wedding and honeymoon over, we settled into married life, new routines and getting used to each other's ways - little things like how we squeeze the toothpaste tube! Martin and John were like chalk and cheese, completely different in many ways. It was a discipline for me not to compare, but to embrace this fresh start; the gratitude of new love enabled us to move forward together with grace and flexibility. I'm certain that if I hadn't had the experience of a second marriage, I would have been quick to judge and spout my opinion about others who find love again after a marriage ends.

Transparency continued to be the watchword in our relationship. Talking things through is so important as we navigate our way through new territory. For instance, John's mum ran a very tight ship in terms of her home-keeping skills. She was of the generation who ironed socks, handkerchiefs and underpants. There was not a speck of dust to be seen in her house - she set the bar high. I could not compete with this level of fastidiousness. We needed a reality check regarding our expectations. One thing about our marriage that was the same as my first time around, was the importance of going to sleep as friends, making sure we had dealt with any grievances before we said goodnight. It's important to realise that no one human being can completely fulfil all our needs and desires. It's unfair to put so much pressure on another person. Only the God who created us, and fully loves and understands us, is able to satisfy our deepest longings.

Our first year of marriage was quite eventful. My parents, now in their 70's moved over from Hull to a bungalow about 10 minutes' drive away from us. John's mum celebrated her 80th birthday. Sadly, just before our first wedding anniversary she suffered a stroke. It was very difficult to see her frustration at being stopped in her tracks. She had prided herself on fulfilling her wedding vows of looking after Allan throughout his illness, and was adamant she could manage without help; consequently, she burned herself out. The local hospital made provision for Allan to reside in the adjacent ward during the time of her recovery and rehabilitation, so he could be near her and visit her regularly. What an amazing blessing that was.

Much to her consternation, we took the opportunity, with Allan's permission, to make some changes to their home. One thing was to install a gas fire to replace the coal fire that she would have to make every morning. She did not appreciate it. I suppose she felt as though she was waving the white flag of surrender, and she was not one for giving in. At Christmas , she was most perturbed that she couldn't make a Christmas cake or pudding. We did a mobile Christmas meal, cooking and delivering the food to eat with them at their house (I think my parents must have spent Christmas with one of my sisters). I can appreciate there is a grieving when one is losing independence and the ability to be in control of one's life.

Another decision with which she struggled enormously was John's decision to leave the bank. This was major for him. He had worked for the bank, albeit in different branches, all his working life, making his way up to management level. You could set your watch by the regularity of his routine. What had caused this uncharacteristic, seemingly rash decision?

My man of integrity had become concerned at the way customers at the bank were being treated. Hard working people having the rug pulled from under them if payments didn't go through in time, and being hit with massive penalties for cash flow issues outside of their control. He was spending more and more of his time giving people debt advice, and trying to help them rather than constructive lending. Then, enough was enough, and he handed in his resignation. When he told his parents of his decision, Hilda was extremely upset with him. A job in the bank was a respectable job for life. She didn't understand his reasons. Fortunately, my Dad and our wise friend Rob were able to visit them on separate occasions and reassure them that all would be well. Once word got out that he was operating as a debt counsellor, he had a string of clients, and went all over the North West of England helping people. Obviously, he could not charge people for his services, but the silver lining of me having been widowed was that the insurance from my first house had meant we were mortgage free, so able to embark on this adventure. I was still working as a part-time teacher, so we were managing to cover our needs.

I was actually not surprised by his decision. A few months before our wedding, we had gone for a walk in the grounds of an old residential school which was up for sale. The church we attended had aspirations of buying it, or being involved with some kind of social care there. When we got back to the car, we were praying about the possibilities. Then John surprised us both with a dangerous prayer: He told God he was willing to leave the bank and be used by Him wherever God wanted Him to serve. Afterwards he looked at me and asked: " Did I really say that?". I think God took him at his word and began to wiggle him out of that comfort zone by bringing about a dissatisfaction with how things at the bank were run.

Sadly, in April, just before her 81st birthday, Hilda suffered a final stroke. She had fought a good fight with dignity and determination, though sometimes we might call it downright stubbornness. John's Dad came to live with us. We turned the dining room into a temporary bedroom, and made plans to convert our attached garage into a proper bedroom for him. Another blessing: John was available to be his Dad's carer. By now, Allan was very unsteady on his feet, requiring a zimmer frame for short distances, and a wheelchair to get out of the house. We determined to get as much support as we could for him. Bless him, he had not had the energy or inclination to remonstrate with his beloved late wife's determination to valiantly battle on alone. She declined every offer of help with defiance. He was a lovely, gentle, mild mannered man. He had survived being a Japanese prisoner of war, and the childhood trauma of being orphaned during the Spanish Flu epidemic following the First World War. I never heard him complain even once about his circumstances.

November has turned out to be a special month for me. After that initial word of encouragement, which I almost completely disregarded, so many important things had happened to me during this season of fruitfulness. November 1992 was no exception.

One bleak November evening, I dragged myself away from the television to go to a prayer meeting at the home of one of our church leaders. A Nigerian couple attended our church, and Folu, the wife, was at this meeting. She said she had an impression that God's fire was burning in someone's stomach. I remembered the prayers of the pastor years ago, when he saw God's healing, cleansing fire burning up the herpes virus in my body. I believed that her word of encouragement was for me. What she didn't know is that John and I had decided it was time for us to try and start a family. A few days earlier, we had gone for a blood test at the hospital to check for the presence of the herpes virus in my blood - there was no trace of it!

I went home and told John. We did the necessary, and straightaway, I knew this was it. "I'll be pregnant!", I said. How could I possibly know?! It's the amazing, wonderful difference when faith has been downloaded. Changed from timid, anxious, doubting to believing and trusting; not in myself, but in God's desire and ability to bless.

A couple of weeks later I woke at 5 a.m. I reached for the pregnancy test in my bedside cupboard and, bleary-eyed, I made my way into the bathroom. John must have sensed my absence in bed and got up to follow me. He was just in time for me to announce: "I've got a double pink line!!" I was pregnant! We shared a relieved and grateful hug. Back to type, just to be sure, I had another test at the pharmacy and then a visit to the doctor - all systems go!

Our trip to see the doctor was quite surreal. This particular doctor was celebrating his final day at the practice and his surgery was festooned with balloons and streamers. There was a party vibe going on, which felt rather fitting for our circumstances. I remember he was wearing a nauseating canary yellow shirt. He offered us his congratulations, then suddenly, as if to steal my thunder, John whipped his sock off and pushed his foot under the doctor's nose, asking him for his opinion on a ganglion by his big toe! It was all very amusing but, strangely, shortly afterwards, the surgery changed their policy to one patient per consultation!

In August 1993 our beautiful daughter Sarah was born. After such a long wait, God's promise to me was finally fulfilled. With hindsight, I realised the promise had been to me, and not to Martin and myself as a couple. The lesson I took from this is to keep on hoping with expectancy, that If God has promised something, He will keep His word.

I was pleased that my parents were able to get to know their new grandchild. Both my older sisters had blessed them with grandchildren, but there was a considerable age gap between our daughter and her cousins. Martin's parents had also been blessed with grandchildren through his sisters. Three years later our family was completed with the arrival of another precious daughter, Anna. Sadly, John's dad didn't get to meet his second granddaughter, but he'd had the joy of becoming a grandpa, even though he must have wondered if he'd ever make it home when he was scrabbling in the dirt down the mines in Burma.

At our wedding ceremony, one of our dear and trusted friends, Steve Hepden, had given us a word of encouragement and promise: that we would be like two rivers running together. Geographically, this was impossible as John hailed from the River Mersey, which is on the west of the country and flows into the Irish Sea, whereas I am from Hull on the River Humber, which is on the east and flows into the North Sea. Metaphorically though, it meant that we two would become one: our molecules would merge, one heart and mind in agreement with each other. It's quite remarkable, as we are so different in many ways. Of course there is a mystery, and a question at the back of the mind about what happens down the line. I've been widowed once, could I handle it again? Well, I am not going to waste these precious days worrying. God gave me the strength and grace before, He will do it again if necessary. I have learned that trials come so that we can press into God and allow him to hone our faith. Diamonds probably look pretty unimpressive when they first emerge from the earth: it's by undergoing the rigours of cutting and polishing, that their true beauty is displayed.

Going back to the river analogy, I expect, like many older couples looking back, young love starts off with the excitement and anticipation of a babbling brook. After many twists and turns, with age and maturity it slows down, but love runs deeper and wider as it supports a variety of life on its way to the wide open sea.

Chapter Fifteen

Pastures New

After several years of working as a voluntary debt advisor, John came across a charity which had recently been birthed in Bradford, West Yorkshire. It was due to his role as church treasurer: he'd been asked to research charities helping people with financial difficulties or suffering hardship, so our church could support them in their valuable work. A telephone call with John Kirkby, founder of Christians Against Poverty (CAP), proved to be life changing for us. The two Johns were both 'singing from the same hymn sheet' in terms of their hearts and methods for helping people in debt crisis. A visit was planned, and subsequently my John was offered a job. He opened up a branch of CAP in our spare room (Allan's old bedroom) and was now getting paid for what he had been doing before for free. Once again, it was amazing to see God's hand at work in our lives. And I have to say, that during those lean years when John wasn't bringing in a wage, we wanted for nothing. If we saw something we wanted to buy, we had to decide if we really needed it, or could we do without it? Actually, that was really freeing. When we did buy something new, it was a real treat, and we treasured it. God was generous to us through other people: we by no means felt as though we were scrimping and scraping. We were able to give the girls lovely family holidays each year, we were given bag fulls of designer clothes for them and we always had food on the table. It has taught us that God truly is our Provision and He is faithful. Our girls too, enjoyed the blessing of being looked after by their Daddy while I was at work part of the week, and then by me when he was doing his client visits or office work.

The tenet of CAP is that clients, if they so desire, are invited to join a local church family where they can be supported and loved. Many clients are so relieved to get their debt under control and connect with people who really care about them in a practical way that they come to have faith in Jesus. The CAP centre John was running in Maghull was not working like that. There were a couple of local people who joined our church, but John was still mostly visiting people right across the North West of England. He was not familiar with churches in those areas, so couldn't guarantee how clients would be supported. We prayed about what to do. We decided that we would leaflet the local council estate, and if we got no feedback, we would know to close down the centre. One lady responded, and John set up a visit, but her husband was dead set against any help, and so that could not be pursued.

After discussions with John Kirkby, John went over to Bradford for a chat. I can remember feeling a bubbling excitement in my tummy, an expectancy that something was afoot. When he returned home, I was in our lovely brand new kitchen extension, making the tea. As he greeted me with a kiss I said to him: "We're moving to Bradford, aren't we?" He grinned with affirmation. He had been asked to help set up and run the new Insolvency Department. It was going to be an adventure for us, although I was a bit gutted that we would leave our lovely home (and brand new kitchen!). We would also have to break the news to my parents. Dad understood but, Mum, understandably, was not best pleased. I felt her pain. I knew she would really miss the joy of seeing her granddaughters on a weekly basis, but John and I were convinced that we were following the path that God was setting out for us.

As is our custom, every important decision is prayed about, and God always confirms His direction for us. He does this in many different ways: usually through a verse in the Bible, or a song or throw-away line someone says without realising its significance. We know that if He has given the go ahead, then we can trust Him and move forward with confidence.

For a few months John travelled over to Bradford for a couple of days a week, and then we set a date to move over permanently. Once again, we saw God's hand at work.

Our girls had been settled and happy at a lovely local Primary school. Over the previous year, the Council had announced that the school was to close, in order to fill spaces at a bigger school in the area. This had been devastating news for the school family. We demonstrated outside the Town Hall, and won a one year reprieve, but that time was now coming to an end, and many parents had panicked about not having new school places for their children. They pulled their children out before the end of term, meaning the girls' school population was so depleted, it was no longer viable to stay open. It was heartbreaking.

We needed to find school places for our daughters, and the village of Idle was recommended to us as a lovely place to live, with a thriving and happy Primary school. Due to all the upset with our previous school, I was feeling quite anxious that we would not be able to secure places for our girls, especially as it was a popular school. Why was I worried?! Amazingly there were two spaces in the appropriate classes for our girls to start in the September. Also, I was able to secure a part-time teaching job at an independent Christian school which was walking distance from our new house. Perfect!

We came over to look for houses in the Spring of that year. John K had told us about a house for sale in the road where he lived. It was literally the only house for sale in the village! Everything else that was suitable was already under offer. It was a huge three-storey Victorian terraced house, with beautiful period features, and big enough to accommodate my parents should the need arise. There was only a small back yard, but the well-used cricket pitch was over the wall at the end of the road. And it was cheaper than the house we'd sold in Maghull! Later, after some family history research by my sister, we discovered that our ancestors had hailed from

Idle several generations back. I had come home, without even realising it. I remember my first trip to the local supermarket after we moved. How lovely to hear those Yorkshire accents again after over twenty years away. I put potted beef and Yorkshire curd tart in my trolley - delicacies I'd missed, that now tasted so good.

There are so many more incidents of God's goodness I could relate, but I would end up telling my whole life story. The bottom line is that God has been, and I believe will continue to be, faithful. And, in case you don't already know it, He will be so for you too.

Not long after our move, my Dad had some difficult news regarding his health: the cancer from which he'd recovered some years back, had returned. He was 'promoted to Glory', but sadly, it left my Mum without family around her. This might seem like a conundrum. How could it have been that God called us over to Bradford leaving my mum in the lurch? (as a family, my sisters and I made sure we were there for her). But God always does have a plan. Although she had good neighbours and a supportive church family in Maghull, Mum expressed her desire to return to Hull. Amazingly, within a few months she was moving into sheltered accommodation in an area she was familiar with from childhood and close to both my sisters. This was certainly a great relief to us all, especially as she was diagnosed with Alzheimers Disease not long after moving. There were a few more challenges ahead regarding Mum's health, but we can look back and see God's provision and strength through it all: she eventually moved to a lovely care home on the edge of a park she frequented during her childhood.

I hope that through everything I've written so far I haven't given the impression that 'things always work out positively and "miraculously" leaving you feeling, "well all this doesn't relate to my circumstances and experiences". But the bottom line is, God sees you, and I believe if you put things in His hands, He will work it out for you.

Chapter Sixteen

Final Thoughts

So, dear Reader, this has been part of my story. I hope that something in these pages has resonated with you. I don't know your griefs and sorrows, but my prayer is that you will feel able to hand them over to the One who is Perfect Love, and allow Him to exchange your pain for peace and hope. He invites you out of the darkness of Winter into the expectancy of Spring.

But let us not forget that even Winter has its own beauty and purpose. There is rest, renewal, transformation going on behind the scenes in the deep and hidden places. We cannot truly appreciate the warmth and beauty of Spring unless we have come through the season of Winter: God uses every experience to enrich us, if we let Him.

After thirty years in teaching, I left to start a small craft business, and one of the things I enjoy most is wet felting. This is the process of turning fleece into felted fabric. When I learned the process I had such a download of parallels with what I had been through, it really excited me. It seems that God uses many creative processes to teach us His reasons for things happening to us: clay in the potter's hand, honing of rough diamonds into precious sparkling gems and the refining of precious metals by heating to draw off impurities, for example.

"The refining pot is for silver, and the furnace for gold, but the LORD tests the hearts." (Proverbs 17:3)

I would like to share briefly with you what I learned through the felting process.

Dyed and carded fleece is laid onto bubble wrap and soaked with warm soapy water, then another layer of bubble wrap is laid on top to make a 'sandwich'. The whole thing is then rolled around a rolling pin and moved backwards and forwards to agitate the fibres. It's the exact motion of making pastry. What happens is amazing: the little barbs on the individual fibres begin to 'reach out' to each other and knit together forming a fabric. This all happens because the fleece has been soaked first in the lubricating soapy water. Without this it would just become a gnarled, knotty mess. After a certain amount of rolling, the fabric is then massaged with extra soap and can be shaped into various forms. The finished felt is a strong, beautiful fabric with its own unique pattern and design - other fibres, such as silk or plant fibres can be added into the fabric during the early stages. There are such powerful messages to be gleaned from this process. How we can reach out to others and be made stronger together, especially those people whom we may not necessarily be comfortable with - God's love extends to all of us, and we can be united as human beings created in His image. Suffering and difficulties are able to produce something beautiful if we submit ourselves into God's hands and allow Him to massage us into His perfect design soaked in His love and the gentle warmth and comfort of the Holy Spirit. God gave me a poem which summarises how the felting process can be a symbol for our suffering:

Work - In - Progress

I am pummelled and stretched, been through the mill,

I don't know how much more I can take of this ill,

Then a Voice: "I know: I am already there!

I'm here right beside you. I do really care!

My Grace, Love and Peace will wash you right through,

You will I beautify, bring forth as new.

Trust me! Something more precious than gold is being wrought,

On a rough wooden Cross your redemption was bought."

Rose Mitchell 2016

Every time I engage in wet felting, or teach others, I am reminded how, before this great 'agitation' and trial came into my life, God prepared me by soaking me continuously in the warm soapy comfort of His word: Jesus promised that those who come to him will receive rivers of living water which will quench their thirst forever. Revelation 1:15 describes His voice as being like the sound of many waters. Ephesians 5:26 tells that we are made clean by being washed by the word of God. Reading the Bible before and during the trial I was going through helped me to gain understanding and comfort. It quenched my thirst for answers as to what was going on. It enabled me to reach out to others and allow them to reach out to me. It made me stronger and I began to see that God had not abandoned me, but had a plan for me. The greatest part of this plan was to cause me to reach out to Him, above all, because, more than anything, that is what He desires: to be in relationship with each one of us. He already knows and created each one of us, but He wants us to come to really know Him and His great, amazing, pure and unconditional love. The love which sent His Son, Jesus, through the greatest trial faced by anyone, ever: to carry the burden of the whole world in order to ransom us from the power of death and sin.

"……Christ.. loved us and gave himself up for us, an offering and a sacrifice to God for a sweet-smelling fragrance." (Ephesians 5:2)

So, in the light of this amazing truth, may I encourage you to trust the One who loves you so passionately and perfectly. Put your future in His hands, because He is the Beginning and the End and everything He has promised in The Bible will come to pass.

God *"will wipe away every tear from their eyes. Death will be no more; neither will there be mourning, nor crying, nor pain anymore. The first things have passed away." He who sits on the throne said, "Behold, I am making all things new." "* (Rev 21:4-5a).

Maybe you are already a follower of Jesus; perhaps disappointment and grief have taken their toll on your faith or you might never have actually got round to thinking about faith before. Whatever your position, I invite you to speak this prayer. It would be good to say it out loud. The words we declare have power:

Father God, thank you that you made me, you know me and love me; you have given me life and designed me for a purpose. I have a destiny. Thank you for sending your Son, Jesus. I acknowledge that He came to the Earth to show me the way back to You. Thank you that He carried all my grief and sorrow, mistakes and failings on the Cross when He died. I receive Him as my Lord and Saviour, and because of His love and forgiveness I am now set free from sin and death. Thank you for the power of the Holy Spirit which raised Jesus to life again: I invite that same Spirit of Truth to fill me up and lead me on this journey. I ask this in the Name of Jesus. Amen.

Well done if you were able to pray that prayer: now do four things:

*Tell someone what you've done.

*Find some other Christians to help you on your journey and seek out a local church community to get involved with.

*Read the Bible. You could download a Bible App if you can't get a physical Bible. Maybe start with the gospels at the beginning of the New Testament.

*Start talking to and listening to Father God/Jesus /Holy Spirit; they are Three in One,(Holy Trinity) so they work together in perfect unity. Just speak normally and share your heart. Don't be afraid to ask questions: be real.

May God bless you on your journey with Him!

Notes

Unless otherwise noted, all Scripture references are taken from WEBBE (World English Bible British Edition), which is in the public domain, and used in adherence to their conditions.

Chapter 8. "Titanic" 1997, Paramount Pictures and Twentieth Century Fox Film Corporation

"I wandered Lonely as a Cloud", William Wordsworth, pub 1807 public domain.

Chapter 9. "Get On Your Feet" 1989, Gloria Estefan, released by Epic Records.

Chapter 10. "Make Way for Christmas-The Gift" 1988 Graham Kendrick, Kingsway.

Chapter 13. "Tell Out My Soul" from Magnificat by Timothy Dudley-Smith 1962.

Acknowledgments

With grateful thanks to all the people who have encouraged and supported me by their acts of kindness, wise words, listening ear or shoulder to cry on over the years. Time, circumstances and distance may have separated us, but I am truly grateful for your input into my life.

Special thanks to my husband, John, for his patient proofreading, supportive advice and encouragement as I incubated this book over many years. Also to Bishop Chris Edmondson for his invaluable assistance and affirmations in helping get this book written and published. Thanks to Anna Mitchell for her skills with the cover design. Finally, thanks to Dave Hopwood, for his generous help in the final stages.

About the Author

After thirty years of teaching, I now enjoy indulging my creativity making gifts and handmade products for my micro business. My main love is felting, which I also enjoy teaching in local workshops. Other passions include cooking, especially for family and friends, and being in nature.

Although, with my husband, I have worshipped in different church traditions, we now are at home at Holy Trinity, Idle where I am involved in discipleship and children's ministry.

I am also blessed by seeing the restoring love of Father God transforming and refreshing people, which is why I am so happy to be involved with ARC Spirit Spa.

To view what I make, search Roseland Creations on Facebook.

Rose Mitchell
2023, Bradford, West Yorkshire

Helpful Organisations and Charities

I have approached these organisations for permission to include them in this list. At the time of publication, not all had replied. Please also note, that my book has not been able to be endorsed by these organisations before its publication. Details correct at time of publishing.

Bereavement support:

Cruse - free helpline: 0808 808 1677; website: www.cruse.org.uk

AtaLoss.org - helpline: 0800 448 0800, provides with helping find bereavement services.

Care for the Family - 029 2081 0800; website: mail@cff.org.uk

Reach Merseyside - 0151 7372121; email: reach@reachuk.co.uk

Financial support:

CAP (Christians Against Poverty) - 01274 761999; website: capuk.org

Childlessness:

Evangelical Movement of Wales - ems.org.uk.

Spiritual Healing:

ARC Spirit Spa - every 2nd & 4th Saturday on Zoom. Email: arc.spirit.spa@gmail.com

Booking: https://arc-spirit-spa.eventbrite.co.uk

Printed in Great Britain
by Amazon